STILL STEAMING

The Guide to Britain's Steam Railways 2004-2005

EDITOR
John Robinson

Eighth Edition

FOREWORD

Following the continued success of Still Steaming in 2003 we have added a number of new locations for this revised 8th edition.

We were greatly impressed by the friendly and cooperative manner of the staff and helpers of the railways which we selected to appear in this book, and wish to thank them all for the help they have given.

Although we believe that the information contained in this guide is accurate at the time of going to press, we, and the Railways and Museums itemised, are unable to accept liability for any loss, damage, distress or injury suffered as a result of any inaccuracies. Furthermore, we and the Railways are unable to guarantee operating and opening times which may always be subject to cancellation without notice.

If you feel we should include other locations or information in future editions, please let us know so that we may give them consideration. We would like to thank you for buying this guide and wish you 'Happy Steaming'.

John Robinson

EDITOR

Note: Further copies of this guide may be obtained, post free, from our address below.

British Library Cataloguing in Publication Data
A catalogue record for this book is available from the British Library

ISBN 1-86223-093-5

Copyright © 2004, MARKSMAN PUBLICATIONS. (01472 696226)
72 St. Peter's Avenue, Cleethorpes, N.E. Lincolnshire, DN35 8HU, England

Printed by The Cromwell Press

CONTENTS

THE FRIENDS OF THE NATIONAL RAILWAY MUSEUM

This organisation was formed in 1977 to help conserve and operate railway exhibits that might otherwise have to wait many years before returning to public view. The organisation is run on a membership basis which imparts a number of privileges which include:

• the *NRM Review*, published quarterly, which keeps Friends in touch with events at the Museum, carries

  information about the National Collection locomotives, features articles of general railway interest and includes authorative reviews of videos and books.

• opportunities to work as a volunteer in the Museum.

• invitations to FNRM members meetings in York and London.

MEMBERSHIP DETAILS – Normal membership is valid for 12 months from date of registration.

Category	Rate
Ordinary	£18.00
Unwaged	£13.50
Junior (Under 18)	£9.00
Family	£27.00
Retired Couple	£20.25
Group	£30.00
Life (below 60)	£ 270.00
Life (60 and over)	£200.00
Life (retired couple)	£300.00
Life (family)	£400.00

Apply for membership to:

FNRM
National Railway Museum
Leeman Road
York
YO26 4XJ

Telephone (01904) 636874

Family Membership – is for a maximum of four persons, two or three of whom are under 18 years of age, residing at the same address

Retired Couple Membership – is for two persons aged 60 or over and not in employment.

Covenanted Membership – if you are a taxpayer, your subscription can be covenanted to produce extra revenue for the Friends. Please ask for more details from the Friends Office.

Charities Aid Foundation – we can accept subscriptions by CAF cheque or CAF charity card.

NATIONAL RAILWAY MUSEUM

Address: National Railway Museum, Leeman Road, York   YO26 4XJ
Telephone Nº: (01904) 621261
Year Formed: 1975
Location of Line: York
Length of Line: Short demonstration line

Nº of Steam Locos: 79
Nº of Other Locos: 37
Approx Nº of Visitors P.A.: 700,000
Web site: www.nrm.org.uk

GENERAL INFORMATION

Nearest Mainline Station: York (¼ mile)
Nearest Bus Station: York (¼ mile)
Car Parking: On site long stay car park
Coach Parking: On site – free to pre-booked groups
Souvenir Shop(s): Yes
Food & Drinks: Yes

SPECIAL INFORMATION

The Museum is the largest of its kind in the world, housing the Nation's collection of locomotives, carriages, uniforms, posters and an extensive photographic archive. Special events and exhibitions run throughout the year. The Museum is the home of the Mallard – the fastest steam locomotive in the world and Shinkansen, the only Bullet train outside of Japan.

OPERATING INFORMATION

Opening Times: Open daily 10.00am to 6.00pm (closed on 24th, 25th and 26th of December)
Steam Working: School holidays – please phone to confirm details
Prices: Free admission for all (excludes some Special events)
Phone (01904) 686263 for further details.

Detailed Directions by Car:
The Museum is located in the centre of York, just behind the Railway Station. It is clearly signposted from all approaches to York.

STEAM RAILWAY LOCATOR MAP

To find the locations of each railway please compare the reference numbers
shown on pages 3-5 with the markers below.
Please note that the markers on this map show the approximate location only.

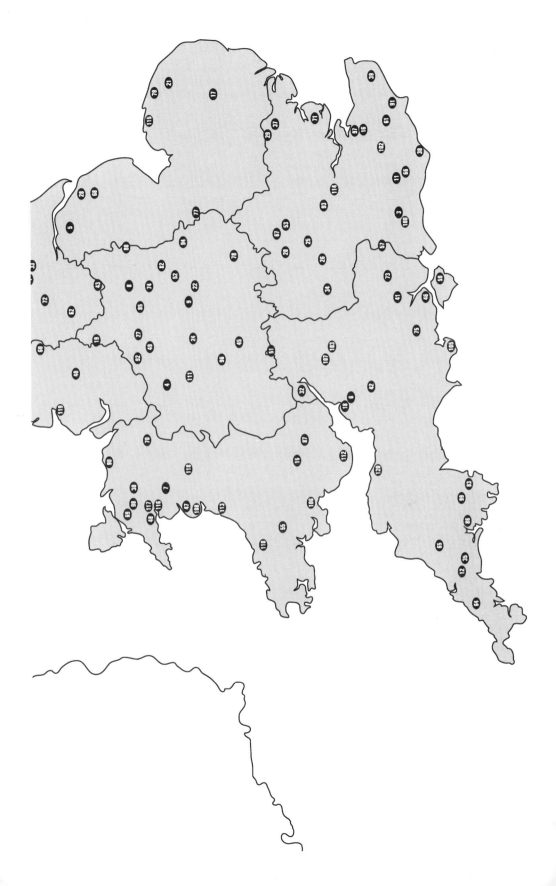

ALFORD VALLEY RAILWAY

Address: Alford Station, Main Street, Alford, Aberdeenshire AB33 8HH	**Nº of Steam Locos:** 1
Telephone Nº: (01975) 562811	**Nº of Other Locos:** 3
Year Formed: 1980	**Nº of Members:** Approximately 70
Location of Line: Alford – Haughton Park	**Annual Membership Fee:** £15.00
Length of Line: 1 mile	**Approx Nº of Visitors P.A.:** 19,500
	Gauge: 2 feet

GENERAL INFORMATION

Nearest Mainline Station: Insch (10 miles)
Nearest Bus Station: Alford (200 yards)
Car Parking: Available on site
Coach Parking: Available on site
Souvenir Shop(s): Yes
Food & Drinks: No

SPECIAL INFORMATION

The Grampian Transport Museum is adjacent to the Railway and the Heritage Centre also has horse-drawn tractors and agricultural machinery.

OPERATING INFORMATION

Opening Times: Weekends in April, May and September. Open daily in June, July and August. Trains run from 1.00pm to 4.30pm
Steam Working: The first Sunday of May, June, July and August only.
Prices: Adult Return £2.00
Child Return £1.00

Detailed Directions by Car:
From All Parts: Alford is situated 25 miles west of Aberdeen on the Highland tourist route. Take the A944 to reach Alford.

AMBERLEY WORKING MUSEUM

Address: Amberley Working Museum, Amberley, Arundel BN18 9LT
Telephone N°: (01798) 831370
Year Formed: 1979
Location of Line: Amberley
Length of Line: ¾ mile

N° of Steam Locos: 3
N° of Other Locos: 20+
N° of Members: 250 volunteers
Annual Membership Fee: £20.00
Approx N° of Visitors P.A.: 60,000
Gauge: 2 feet

GENERAL INFORMATION

Nearest Mainline Station: Amberley (adjacent)
Nearest Bus Station: –
Car Parking: Free parking available on site
Coach Parking: Free parking available on site
Souvenir Shop(s): Yes
Food & Drinks: Yes

SPECIAL INFORMATION

Amberley Working Museum covers 36 acres of former chalk pits and consists of over 30 buildings containing hundreds of different exhibits.

OPERATING INFORMATION

Opening Times: Wednesday to Sunday from 17th March to 31st October and also on Bank Holidays. Trains run from 10.00am to 5.30pm
Steam Working: Please phone for details.
Prices: Adult £7.50
Child £4.30 (free for Under-5's)
Family £20.00 (2 adults + 3 children)

Web site: www.amberleymuseum.co.uk

Detailed Directions by Car:
From All Parts: Amberley Working Museum is situated in West Sussex on the B2139 mid-way between Arundel and Storrington and is adjacent to Amberley Railway Station.

AMERTON RAILWAY

Address: Amerton Farm, Stow-by-Chartley, Staffordshire ST18 0LA
Telephone N°: (01785) 850965
Year Formed: 1991
Location: Amerton Farm
Length of Line: Approximately 1 mile

N° of Steam Locos: 3
N° of Other Locos: 7
N° of Members: 45
Approx N° of Visitors P.A.: 30,000
Gauge: 2 feet
Web site: www.amertonrailway.co.uk

GENERAL INFORMATION

Nearest Mainline Station: Stafford (8 miles)
Nearest Bus Station: Stafford (8 miles)
Car Parking: Free parking available on site
Coach Parking: Available by arrangement
Souvenir Shop(s): Yes
Food & Drinks: Yes

SPECIAL INFORMATION

The Railway is run by volunteers and the circuit was completed in 2002.

OPERATING INFORMATION

Opening Times: Weekends from early April to the end of October and on Tuesdays and Thursdays during School Holidays. Also open for Santa Specials in December. Open from midday to 5.00pm
Steam Working: Sundays and Bank Holidays only.
Prices: Adult £1.50
Child 90p
Concession £1.20
Family Ticket £4.00

Detailed Directions by Car:
Amerton is located on the A518, 1 mile from the junction with the A51 – Amerton Farm is signposted at the junction. The Railway is located approximately 8 miles from Junction 14 of the M6.

APPLEBY FRODINGHAM RAILWAY

Address: Appleby Frodingham Railway Preservation Society, P.O. Box 44, Brigg, North Lincolnshire   DN20 8DW
Telephone Nº: (01652) 656661
Year Formed: 1990
Location of Line: Corus Steelworks, Scunthorpe

Length of Line: 18 miles of track
Nº of Steam Locos: 3
Nº of Other Locos: 2
Nº of Members: 60
Annual Membership Fee: –
Gauge: Standard
Web site: www.afrps.co.uk

GENERAL INFORMATION

Nearest Mainline Station: Scunthorpe (2 miles)
Nearest Bus Station: Scunthorpe (2 miles)
Car Parking: Large free car park at the site
Coach Parking: At the site
Souvenir Shop(s): Yes – at the Loco Shed
Food & Drinks: Drinks/snacks served on train trips

SPECIAL INFORMATION

A selection of Rail tours and Brake Van tours are operated over a distance of 7 to 18 miles of the steelworks internal railway system.

OPERATING INFORMATION

Opening Times: Selected weekends throughout the year which must be pre-booked via (01652) 657053 or e-mail – bookings@afrps.co.uk
Steam Working: See above
Prices: Free – but donations are accepted
Please note that children cannot be carried on Brake van tours due to the open verandahs.

Detailed Directions by Car:
Exit the M180 at Junction 3 onto the M181, at the end turn right onto the A18. Take the 3rd exit at the rounda-bout (still on the A18) and turn left onto Ashby Road at the next roundabout. At the following roundabout turn right into Rowland Road and at the end of the road turn right then left into Entrance E. Car parking is available on the left and the path to the station is on the right.

AVON VALLEY RAILWAY

Address: Bitton Station, Bath Road, Bitton, Bristol BS30 6HD	**Nº of Steam Locos:** 6
Telephone Nº: (0117) 932-7296	**Nº of Other Locos:** 3
Year Formed: 1973	**Nº of Members:** Approximately 500
Location of Line: Midway between Bristol and Bath on A431	**Annual Membership Fee:** £13.00
	Approx Nº of Visitors P.A.: 80,000
Length of Line: 3 miles	**Gauge:** Standard
	Web site: www.avonvalleyrailway.co.uk

GENERAL INFORMATION

Nearest Mainline Station: Keynsham (1½ miles)
Nearest Bus Station: Bristol or Bath (7 miles)
Car Parking: Available at Bitton Station
Coach Parking: Available at Bitton Station
Souvenir Shop(s): Yes
Food & Drinks: Yes

SPECIAL INFORMATION

The line has been extended through the scenic Avon Valley towards Bath and a new platform is now open.

OPERATING INFORMATION

Opening Times: Every Sunday from Easter to October and on weekends during December. Also Bank Holiday Mondays and Tuesdays to Thursdays from 20th July to 26th August. Also open for Santa Specials over Christmas. Open 10.30am to 5.00pm.
Steam Working: 11.00am to 4.00pm
Prices: Adult £4.50
        Child £3.00
        Family Tickets £12.50
        Senior Citizens £3.50

Detailed Directions by Car:
From All Parts: Exit the M4 at Junction 18. Follow the A46 towards Bath and at the junction with the A420 turn right towards Bristol. At Bridge Yate turn left onto the A4175 and continue until you reach the A431. Turn right and Bitton Station is 100 yards on the right.

BALA LAKE RAILWAY

Address: Bala Lake Railway, Llanuwchllyn, Gwynedd, LL23 7DD	**No of Steam Locos**: 4
Telephone No: (01678) 540666	**No of Other Locos**: –
Year Formed: 1972	**No of Members**: –
Location of Line: Llanuwchllyn to Bala	**Approx No of Visitors P.A.**: 20,000
Length of Line: 4½ miles	**Gauge**: 1 foot 11 five-eighth inches
	Web site: www.bala-lake-railway.co.uk

GENERAL INFORMATION

Nearest Mainline Station: Wrexham (40 miles)
Nearest Bus Station: Wrexham (40 miles)
Car Parking: Adequate parking in Llanuwchllyn
Coach Parking: At Llanuwchllyn or in Bala Town Centre
Souvenir Shop(s): Yes
Food & Drinks: Yes – unlicensed!

SPECIAL INFORMATION

Bala Lake Railway is a narrow-gauge railway which follows 4½ miles of the former Ruabon to Barmouth G.W.R. line.

OPERATING INFORMATION

Opening Times: 3rd April to 3rd October.
Steam Working: All advertised services are steam hauled. Trains run from 11.15am to 4.00pm.
Prices: Adult Single £4.00; Return £6.70
Child Single £2.00; Return £3.00
Senior Citizen Return £6.20
Family Tickets (Return): £8.00 (1 Adult + 1 Child); £16.00 (2 Adults + 2 Children). Additional Children are £1.50 each. Under 5's travel free of charge.

Detailed Directions by Car:
From All Parts: The railway is situated off the A494 Bala to Dolgellau road which is accessible from the national motorways via the A5 or A55.

BARROW HILL ROUNDHOUSE RAILWAY CENTRE

Address: Barrow Hill Roundhouse, Campbell Drive, Barrow Hill, Chesterfield S43 2PR	**N° of Steam Locos**: 7
Telephone N°: (01246) 472450	**N° of Other Locos**: Over 40
Year Formed: 1998	**N° of Members**: Approximately 400
Location: Staveley, near Chesterfield	**Annual Membership Fee**: £13.00 Adult
Length of Line: ¾ mile	**Approx N° of Visitors P.A.**: 30,000
	Gauge: Standard
	Web site: www.barrowhill.org.uk

GENERAL INFORMATION

Nearest Mainline Station: Chesterfield (3½ miles)
Nearest Bus Station: Chesterfield (3 miles)
Car Parking: Space available for 100 cars
Coach Parking: Available
Souvenir Shop(s): Yes
Food & Drinks: Yes – buffet

SPECIAL INFORMATION

Britain's last remaining operational Railway roundhouse provides storage and repair facilities for standard gauge locomotives and diesels.

OPERATING INFORMATION

Opening Times: Open at weekends throughout the year from 10.00am to 4.30pm (for static viewing).
Steam Working: Special open days only – Steam Gala on 9th & 10th October; Santa Steam Trains on 5th, 12th and 19th December.
Prices: Please phone for prices
Note: Driver training courses are available – please phone for further details.

Detailed Directions by Car:
Exit the M1 at Junction 30 and take the A619 to Staveley (about 3½ miles). Pass through Staveley, turn right at Troughbrook onto 'Works Road'. Continue along for ¾ mile, pass under the railway bridge and take the turn immediately on the right. Turn left onto Campbell Drive and the Roundhouse is behind Acorn Van Hire.

THE BATTLEFIELD LINE

Address: The Battlefield Line,
Shackerstone Station, Shackerstone,
Warwickshire   CV13 6NW
Telephone Nº: (01827) 880754
Year Formed: 1968
Location of Line: North West of Market
Bosworth
Length of Line: 5 miles

Nº of Steam Locos: 5
Nº of Other Locos: 20
Nº of Members: 500 approximately
Annual Membership Fee: £15.00 Adult;
£20.00 Family
Approx Nº of Visitors P.A.: 50,000
Gauge: Standard

GENERAL INFORMATION

Nearest Mainline Station: Nuneaton (9 miles)
Nearest Bus Station: Nuneaton & Hinckley (9 miles)
Car Parking: Ample free parking available
Coach Parking: Can cater for coach parties
Souvenir Shop(s): Yes
Food & Drinks: Yes – Station Buffet

SPECIAL INFORMATION

Travel from the Grade II listed Shackerstone Station
through the beautiful Leicestershire countryside
with views of the adjoining Ashby Canal. Arrive at
the award-winning Shenton Station and explore
Bosworth Battlefield (1485) before making the
return journey.

OPERATING INFORMATION

Operating Info: 9th April to the 31st October and
Santa Specials during December. Please telephone
for further details
Opening Times: 10.30am to 6.00pm
Steam Working: From 11.15am to 4.15pm during
high season and Sundays.
Prices: Adult Return £7.00
        Child Return £4.00
        O.A.P. Return £5.00
        Family Ticket £18.00
        (2 adults and 2 children)

Detailed Directions by Car:
Follow the brown tourist signs from the A444 or A447 heading towards the market town of Market Bosworth.
Continue towards the villages of Congerstone & Shackerstone and finally to Shackerstone Station. Access is only
available via the Old Trackbed.

BEAMISH – THE NORTH OF ENGLAND OPEN AIR MUSEUM

Address: Beamish North of England Open Air Museum, Co. Durham DH9 0RG **Telephone No:** (0191) 370-4000 **Year Formed:** 1970 **Length of Line:** ½ mile	**No of Steam Locos:** 10 **No of Other Locos:** 4 **N.B.:** Not all Locos are on display **Approx No of Visitors P.A.:** 320,000 **Web site:** www.beamish.org.uk

GENERAL INFORMATION

Nearest Mainline Station: Newcastle Central (8 miles); Durham City (12 miles)
Nearest Bus Station: Durham (12 miles), Newcastle (8 miles)
Car Parking: Free parking for 2,000 cars
Coach Parking: Free parking for 40 coaches
Souvenir Shop(s): Yes
Food & Drinks: Yes – self service tea room & licensed period Public House. Coffee shop in Summer.

SPECIAL INFORMATION

The Steam Elephant, a magnificent, full-size working replica of an early 'lost' locomotive from the 1800's (pictured left), made it's debut in 2002. This amazing locomotive is in action during the Summer season, alongside a replica of Locomotion No 1, taking visitors on a short ride along the Museum's 1825 Railway.

OPERATING INFORMATION

Opening Times: Open all year round from 10.00am to 4.00pm in the Winter – open until 5.00 during the Summer. Closed Mondays and Fridays in the Winter.
N.B. Winter visits are centred on the Town and Tramway only. Other areas are closed and admission prices are reduced.
Allow 4-5 hours for a Summer visit and two hours in the Winter.
Steam Working: Daily during the Summer
Prices:
Adult £14.00 in Summer; £5.00 in Winter
Child £7.00 in Summer; £5.00 in Winter
O.A.P. £11.00 in Summer; £5.00 in Winter
Children under 5 are admitted free.

Detailed Directions by Car:
From North & South: Follow the A1(M) to Junction 63 (Chester-le-street) and then take A693 for 4 miles towards Stanley; From North-West: Take the A68 south to Castleside near Consett and follow the signs on the A692 and A693 via Stanley.

THE BLUEBELL RAILWAY

Address: The Bluebell Railway, Sheffield Park Station, Nr. Uckfield, East Sussex, TN22 3QL
Telephone Nº: (01825) 720800
Information Line: (01825) 722370
Year Formed: 1959
Location of Line: Nr. Uckfield, E. Sussex
Length of Line: 9 miles

Nº of Steam Locos: Over 30 with up to 3 in operation on any given day
Nº of Other Locos: –
Nº of Members: 8,000
Annual Membership Fee: £17.00 Adult
Approx Nº of Visitors P.A.: 175,000
Gauge: Standard
Web site: www.bluebell-railway.co.uk

GENERAL INFORMATION

Nearest Mainline Station: East Grinstead (2 miles) with a bus connection
Nearest Bus Station: East Grinstead
Car Parking: Parking at Sheffield Park and Horsted Keynes Stations.
Coach Parking: Sheffield Park is best
Souvenir Shop(s): Yes
Food & Drinks: Yes – buffets and licensed bars & restaurant

SPECIAL INFORMATION

The Railway runs 'Golden Arrow' dining trains on Saturday evenings and Sunday lunchtimes. There is also a museum and model railway at Sheffield Park Station.

OPERATING INFORMATION

Opening Times: Open every weekend and also daily from May to September inclusive. Also open during School holidays and Santa Specials during December. Open from approximately 10.30am to 5.30pm
Steam Working: As above
Prices: Adult Return £9.00
Child Return £4.50
Family Return £25.00 (2 adult + 3 child)
Senior Citizen Return £7.50

Detailed Directions by Car:
Sheffield Park Station is situated on the A275 Wych Cross to Lewes road. Horsted Keynes Station is signposted from the B2028 Lingfield to Haywards Heath road.

BODMIN & WENFORD RAILWAY

Address: Bodmin General Station, Losthwithiel Road, Bodmin, Cornwall PL31 1AQ	**Length of Line:** 6½ miles
	No of Steam Locos: 10
	No of Other Locos: 9
Telephone No: (0845) 1259678	**No of Members:** 850
Year Formed: 1984	**Annual Membership Fee:** £10.00
Location of Line: Bodmin Parkway Station to Bodmin General & Boscarne Junction.	**Approx No of Visitors P.A.:** 50,000
	Gauge: Standard

GENERAL INFORMATION

Nearest Mainline Station: Bodmin Parkway
Nearest Bus Station: Bodmin (¼ mile)
Car Parking: Free parking at site
Coach Parking: Free parking at site
Souvenir Shop(s): Yes
Food & Drinks: Yes

SPECIAL INFORMATION

The Railway has steep gradients and there are two different branches to choose from Bodmin General. Through tickets to "Bodmin & Wenford Railway" are available from all Mainline stations.

Web site: www.bodminandwenfordrailway.co.uk

OPERATING INFORMATION

Opening Times: Daily from 29th May to the end of September. Also daily during Easter – 3rd to 18th April. Open selected dates from March – May + October and also for Santa Specials in December. Approximately 10.00am to 5.00pm but also during the evenings in the Summer.

Steam Working: Usually trains are steam-hauled except for most Saturdays when Diesels are used.

Prices: Adult Return £5.00 to £9.00
Child Return £3.00 to £5.00
Family Return £14.50 to £25.00
(2 adults + up to 4 children)

Detailed Directions by Car:
From the A30/A38 follow the signs to Bodmin Town Centre then follow the brown tourist signs to the Steam Railway on the B3268 Losthwithiel Road.

BO'NESS & KINNEIL RAILWAY

Address: Bo'ness Station, Union Street, Bo'ness, West Lothian EH51 9AQ	**N° of Steam Locos**: 21
Telephone N°: (01506) 822298	**N° of Other Locos**: 18
Year Opened: 1981	**N° of Members**: 1,300
Location of Line: Bo'ness to Birkhill	**Annual Membership Fee**: £14.00
Length of Line: 3½ miles	**Approx N° of Visitors P.A.**: 60,000
	Gauge: Standard

GENERAL INFORMATION

Nearest Mainline Station: Linlithgow (3 miles)
Nearest Bus Station: Bo'ness (¼ mile)
Car Parking: Free parking at Bo'ness and Birkhill Stations
Coach Parking: Free parking at Bo'ness Station
Souvenir Shop(s): Yes
Food & Drinks: Yes

SPECIAL INFORMATION

The Scottish Railway Exhibition is situated at Bo'ness and conducted tours are also available of the caverns of Birkhill Mine.

OPERATING INFORMATION

Opening Times: Open on weekends from April to October. Also open daily from 3rd July to 30th August with diesels only running on Mondays.
Steam Working: The first train leaves at 11.00am and is steam-hauled as are all trains during the day. The last train leaves at 4.15pm and is diesel-hauled.
Prices: Adult Return £4.50   Child Return £2.00
Family Return £11.00   Concession Return £3.50
N.B. Group discounts are also available – please phone for further details. Also, special fares and timetables apply for special events.

Detailed Directions by Car:
From Edinburgh: Take the M9 and exit at Junction 3. Then take the A904 to Bo'ness; From Glasgow: Take the M80 to M876 and then M9 (South). Exit at Junction 5 and take A904 to Bo'ness; From the North: Take M9 (South), exit at Junction 5, then take A904 to Bo'ness; From Fife: Leave the A90 after the Forth Bridge, then take A904 to Bo'ness.

BOWES RAILWAY

Address: Bowes Railway, Springwell Village, Gateshead, Tyne & Wear NE9 7QJ **Telephone Nº**: (0191) 416-1847 **Year Formed**: 1976 **Location of Line**: Springwell Village **Length of Line**: 1¼ miles	**Nº of Steam Locos**: 2 **Nº of Other Locos**: 4 **Nº of Members**: Approximately 70 **Annual Membership Fee**: £12.00 **Approx Nº of Visitors P.A.**: 5,000 **Gauge**: Standard

GENERAL INFORMATION

Nearest Mainline Station: Newcastle Central (3 miles)
Nearest Bus Station: Gateshead Interchange (2 miles)
Car Parking: Free parking at site
Coach Parking: Free parking at site
Souvenir Shop(s): Yes
Food & Drinks: Yes

SPECIAL INFORMATION

Designed by George Stephenson and opened in 1826, the Railway is a scheduled Ancient Monument which operates unique preserved standard gauge rope-hauled inclines and steam hauled passenger trains.

OPERATING INFORMATION

Opening Times: During 2004: 2nd May; 13th June; 4th July; 1st August; 5th September; 3rd October. Also pre-booked only Santa Specials on 4th, 5th & 12th December.
Steam Working: Every 45 minutes from 12.00pm to 3.55pm.
Prices: Adult Return £3.00
Child Return £1.50
Senior Citizens £1.50
(Prices include a train ride and a demonstration of the Rope Haulage inclines)

Web site: www.bowesrailway.co.uk

Detailed Directions by Car:
From A1 (Northbound): Follow the A194(M) to the Tyne Tunnel and turn left at the sign for Springwell; From A1 (Southbound): Take the turn off left for the B1288 to Springwell and Wrekenton.

BRECON MOUNTAIN RAILWAY

Address: Pant Station, Dowlais, Merthyr Tydfil CF48 2UP	**Length of Line:** 3½ miles
Telephone Nº: (01685) 722988	**Nº of Steam Locos:** 8
Year Formed: 1980	**Nº of Other Locos:** 1
Location of Line: North of Merthyr Tydfil – 1 mile from the A465	**Nº of Members:** –
	Annual Membership Fee: –
	Approx Nº of Visitors P.A.: 70,000
Gauge: 1 foot 11¾ inches	**Web site:** www.breconmountainrailway.co.uk

GENERAL INFORMATION

Nearest Mainline Station: Merthyr Tydfil (3 miles)
Nearest Bus Station: Merthyr Tydfil (3 miles)
Car Parking: Available at Pant Station
Coach Parking: Available at Pant Station
Souvenir Shop(s): Yes
Food & Drinks: Yes – including licensed restaurant

SPECIAL INFORMATION

It is possible to take a break before the return journey at Pontsticill to have a picnic, take a forest walk or visit the lakeside snackbar.

OPERATING INFORMATION

Opening Times: Daily from 27th March to 31st October. Closed on some Mondays and Fridays in April, May, September and October.
Steam Working: 11.00am to 4.00pm
Prices: Adult Return £7.50
  Child Return (15 and under) £3.75
  Senior Citizen Return £6.80
  Dogs or Bicycles £1.50
  Family Rate – The first two children can travel for £2.50 each when accompanied by an adult.

Detailed Directions by Car:
Exit the M4 at Junction 32 and take the A470 to Merthyr Tydfil. Go onto the A465 and follow the brown tourist signs for the railway.

BREDGAR & WORMSHILL LIGHT RAILWAY

Address: The Warren, Bredgar, near Sittingbourne, Kent ME9 8AT	**Nº of Steam Locos:** 13
Telephone Nº: (01622) 884254	**Nº of Other Locos:** 1
Year Formed: 1972	**Nº of Members:** –
Location of Line: 1 mile south of Bredgar	**Annual Membership Fee:** –
Gauge: 1 foot 11¾ inches	**Approx Nº of Visitors P.A.:** 7,000
Length of Line: ½ mile	**Web site:** www.bwlr.co.uk

GENERAL INFORMATION

Nearest Mainline Station:
Hollingbourne (3 miles) or Sittingbourne (5 miles)
Nearest Bus Station: Sittingbourne
Car Parking: 500 spaces available – free parking
Coach Parking: Free parking available by appointment
Souvenir Shop(s): Yes
Food & Drinks: Yes

SPECIAL INFORMATION

A small but beautiful railway in rural Kent. The railway also has other attractions including a Model Railway, Traction Engines, a working Beam Engine, Vintage cars, a Locomotive Shed, a picnic site and woodland walks.

OPERATING INFORMATION

Opening Times: Open on the first Sunday of the month from May to October. Open from 10.30am to 5.00pm
Steam Working: 11.00am to 4.30pm
Prices: Adult £6.00 Child £3.00

Detailed Directions by Car:
Take the M20 and exit at Junction 8 (Leeds Castle exit). Travel 4½ miles due north through Hollingbourne. The Railway is situated a little over 1 mile south of Bredgar village.

BRESSINGHAM STEAM EXPERIENCE

Address: Bressingham Steam Museum, Bressingham, Diss, Norfolk IP22 2AB	**Nº of Steam Locos**: Many Steam locos
Telephone Nº: (01379) 686900	**Nº of Other Locos**: –
Year Formed: Mid 1950's	**Nº of Members**: 70 volunteers
Location of Line: Bressingham, Near Diss	**Annual Membership Fee**: –
Length of Line: 5 miles in total (3 lines)	**Approx Nº of Visitors P.A.**: 90,000+
	Gauge: Standard & 3 Narrow gauge lines

GENERAL INFORMATION

Nearest Mainline Station: Diss (2½ miles)
Nearest Bus Station: Bressingham (1¼ miles)
Car Parking: Free parking for 400 cars available
Coach Parking: Free parking for 30 coaches
Souvenir Shop(s): Yes
Food & Drinks: Yes

SPECIAL INFORMATION

In addition to Steam locomotives, Bressingham has a large selection of steam traction engines, fixed steam engines and also the National Dad's Army Museum, two extensive gardens and a water garden centre.

Web site: www.bressingham.co.uk

OPERATING INFORMATION

Opening Times: Daily from 29th March to the end of September 10.30am to 5.30pm. Daily in October from 10.30 to 4.30pm.
Steam Working: All days, but 'Full Steam' days on Thursdays and Sundays have more trains and steam demonstrations running.
Prices: Adult £7.50
                   Child £5.00
                   Family £18.00
                   Senior Citizens & Students £6.50
Prices shown are for High Season – Low Season prices are slightly lower.

Detailed Directions by Car:
From All Parts: Take the A11 to Thetford and then follow the A1066 towards Diss for Bressingham. The Museum is signposted by the brown tourist signs.

BRISTOL HARBOUR RAILWAY

Address: Bristol Industrial Museum, Princes Wharf, City Docks, Bristol, BS1 4RN	**Length of Line**: 1½ miles
	Nº of Steam Locos: 2
	Nº of Other Locos: 1
Telephone Nº: (0117) 925-1470	**Nº of Members**: –
Year Formed: 1978	**Annual Membership Fee**: –
Location of Line: South side of the Floating Harbour	**Approx Nº of Visitors P.A.**: 70,000
	Gauge: Standard

GENERAL INFORMATION

Nearest Mainline Station: Bristol Temple Meads (1 mile)
Nearest Bus Station: City Centre (½ mile)
Car Parking: Parking available at site
Coach Parking: Drop off and Pick up only
Souvenir Shop(s): Yes
Food & Drinks: Cafes available near the Railway

SPECIAL INFORMATION

The Railway is one of the attractions of the Bristol Industrial Museum which has over 400 exhibits to see, housed in historic transit sheds by a dockside location.

OPERATING INFORMATION

Opening Times: Saturday to Wednesday throughout the year. Opens from 10.00am – 5.00pm
Steam Working: 2004 dates: March 27/28; April 10/11/12/24/25; May 1/2/3/15/16/29/30/31; June 12/13/26/27; July 10/11/24/25/31; August 1/28/29/30; September 11/12/25/26; October 9/10/23/24/30/31.
Prices: Return £1.00
Single 60p
Family Ticket: £3.50
(Children under 6 travel for free)
N.B. Admission to the Museum is free of charge.

Detailed Directions by Car:
From All Parts: Follow signs to Bristol City Centre and then the Brown Tourist signs for the Museum. A good landmark to look out for are the 4 huge quayside cranes.

BROOKSIDE MINIATURE RAILWAY

Address: Macclesfield Road (A523), Poynton, Cheshire SK12 1BY	**Nº of Steam Locos:** 5
Telephone Nº: (01625) 872919	**Nº of Other Locos:** 3
Year Formed: 1989	**Nº of Members:** –
Location: Brookside Garden Centre	**Approx Nº of Visitors P.A.:** 120,000
Length of Line: Approximately ½ mile	**Gauge:** 7¼ inches
	Web: www.brookside-miniature-railway.co.uk

GENERAL INFORMATION

Nearest Mainline Station: Poynton and Hazel Grove (both 1 mile)
Nearest Bus Station: Stockport (5 miles).
Car Parking: 400 spaces available on site
Coach Parking: 2 spaces available
Souvenir Shop(s): Yes
Food & Drinks: Yes

SPECIAL INFORMATION

The Railway runs through the grounds of the Brookside Garden Centre. There is also an extensive collection of Railwayana on display.

OPERATING INFORMATION

Opening Times: Railway is open weekends and Bank Holidays plus Wednesdays from March to September. Open every day in July and August. Trains usually run from 10.45am to 4.30pm but only until 4.00pm from November to February.
Steam Working: Weekends and Bank Holidays only
Prices: Adult £1.00 per ride (10 ride tickets £8.00)
Child 50p per ride (10 ride tickets £4.00)

Detailed Directions by Car:
From the North: Exit the M60 at Junction 1 in Stockport and take the A6 (signposted Buxton). Upon reaching Hazel Grove, take the A523 to Poynton. Follow the brown tourist signs for the Railway; From the West: Exit the M56 at Junction 6 signposted Wilmslow and continue to Poynton. Follow the brown signs for the Railway; From the South: Exit the M6 at Junction 18 for Holmes Chapel. Follow the signs to Wilmslow, then as from the West; From the East: Follow the A6 to Hazel Grove, then as from the North.

BUCKINGHAMSHIRE RAILWAY CENTRE

Address: Quainton Road Station, Quainton, Aylesbury, Bucks. HP22 4BY	**Nº of Steam Locos**: 30
Telephone Nº: (01296) 655720	**Nº of Other Locos**: 6
Year Formed: 1969	**Nº of Members**: 1,000
Location of Line: At Quainton on the old Metropolitan/Great Central Line	**Annual Membership Fee**: £15.00
	Approx Nº of Visitors P.A.: 40,000
	Gauge: Standard
Length of Line: 2 × ½ mile demo tracks	**Recorded Info. Line**: (01296) 655450

GENERAL INFORMATION

Nearest Mainline Station: Aylesbury (6 miles)
Nearest Bus Station: Aylesbury
Car Parking: Free parking for 500 cars available
Coach Parking: Free parking for 10 coaches
Souvenir Shop(s): Yes
Food & Drinks: Yes

SPECIAL INFORMATION

In addition to a large collection of locomotives and carriages, the Centre has an extensive outdoor miniature railway system. The former LNWR Oxford Bewley Road Station is now a visitor centre.

Web site: www.bucksrailcentre.org.uk

OPERATING INFORMATION

Opening Times: Wednesday to Sunday and Bank Holidays from March to October. Open from 10.30am to 4.30pm.
Steam Working: Sundays and Bank Holidays from April to October and also on Wednesdays during June, July, August and the School holidays.
Prices: Adult £6.00 – £7.00
Child £4.00 – £5.00
(Under 5's Free of charge)
Senior Citizen £4.00 – £5.00
Family £18.00 – £20.00
(2 adults + up to 4 children)

Detailed Directions by Car:
The Buckinghamshire Railway Centre is signposted off the A41 Aylesbury to Bicester Road at Waddesdon and off the A413 Buckingham to Aylesbury road at Whitchurch. Junctions 7, 8 and 9 of the M40 are all close by.

BURE VALLEY RAILWAY

Address: Aylsham Station, Norwich Road, Aylsham, Norfolk NR11 6BW
Telephone N°: (01263) 733858
Year Formed: 1989
Location of Line: Between Aylsham & Wroxham
Length of Line: 9 miles

N° of Steam Locos: 5
N° of Other Locos: 3
Approx N° of Visitors P.A.: 127,000
Gauge: 15 inches
Web Site: www.bvrw.co.uk
e-mail: info@bvrw.co.uk

GENERAL INFORMATION

Nearest Mainline Station: Wroxham (adjacent)
Nearest Bus Station: Aylsham (bus passes station)
Car Parking: Free parking at Aylsham & Wroxham Stations
Coach Parking: As above
Souvenir Shop(s): Yes at both Stations
Food & Drinks: Yes (also a Restaurant at Aylsham)

SPECIAL INFORMATION

Boat trains connect at Wroxham with 1½ hour cruise on the Norfolk Broads. Steam Locomotive driving courses are available in off-peak periods.

OPERATING INFORMATION

Opening Times: Various dates from 15th February to 31st October. Daily from 4th April to 26th September. Trains run from 10.15am to 5.15pm most days when open.
Steam Working: Most trains are steam hauled
Prices: Adult Return £8.50 (Single £5.50)
Child Return £5.00 (Single £4.00)
Senior Cit. Return £8.00 (Single £5.00)
Family Return £25.00 (2 adult + 2 child)
Some Carriages have special facilities to carry wheelchairs. Party discounts are available for groups of 20 or more if booked in advance.

Detailed Directions by Car:
From Norwich: Aylsham Station is midway between Norwich and Cromer on the A140 – follow the Aylsham Town Centre signs. Wroxham Station is adjacent to the Wroxham British Rail Station – take the A1151 from Norwich; From King's Lynn: Take A148 and B1354 to reach Aylsham Station.

CADEBY LIGHT RAILWAY

Address: The Old Rectory, Cadeby, Nuneaton, Warks. CV13 0AS
Telephone N°: (01455) 290462
Year Formed: 1961
Location of Line: 1 mile from Market Bosworth, 6 miles from Hinckley
Length of Line: 75 yards

N° of Steam Locos: 3
N° of Other Locos: 15
N° of Members: –
Annual Membership Fee: –
Approx N° of Visitors P.A.: –
Gauge: 2 feet

GENERAL INFORMATION

Nearest Mainline Station: Hinckley (6 miles)
Nearest Bus Station: Market Bosworth (1 mile)
Car Parking: Free parking at site
Coach Parking: Roadside parking
Souvenir Shop(s): Yes
Food & Drinks: Yes

SPECIAL INFORMATION

A new museum was opened in 1990, 'The Boston Collection', encompassing the lifetime collection of the late Reverend Teddy Boston and his family. The narrow gauge railway running in the grounds of the old rectory has been saved by Teddy Boston's widow and a small band of dedicated supporters.

OPERATING INFORMATION

Opening Times: 2nd Saturday of selected months plus specials – please phone for details.
Steam Working: As above.
Prices: Free, but donations are requested.

Detailed Directions by Car:
Exit the M1 at Junction 18 and take the A5 to Hinckley. From Hinckley take the A447 to Cadeby.

CALEDONIAN RAILWAY

Address: The Station, 2 Park Road, Brechin, Angus DD9 7AF	**No of Steam Locos**: 10
Telephone No: (01561) 377760	**No of Other Locos**: 12
Year Formed: 1979	**No of Members**: 250
Location of Line: From Brechin to Bridge of Dun	**Annual Membership Fee**: Adult £12.00; Family £15.00; OAP/Junior £5.00
Length of Line: 4 miles	**Approx No of Visitors P.A.**: 12,000
	Gauge: Standard
	Web site: www.caledonianrailway.co.uk

GENERAL INFORMATION

Nearest Mainline Station: Montrose (4½ miles)
Nearest Bus Station: Brechin (200 yards)
Car Parking: Ample free parking at both Stations
Coach Parking: Free parking at both Stations
Souvenir Shop(s): Yes
Food & Drinks: Light refreshments are available

SPECIAL INFORMATION

Brechin Station is the only original Terminus station in preservation.

OPERATING INFORMATION

Opening Times: Open Easter Sunday, the three Sundays before Christmas and every Sunday from 30th May to 5th September. Also open on other dates.
Steam Working: Steam service on every Sunday.
Prices: Adult Return £5.00
Child Return £3.00
Senior Citizen Return £4.00
Family Return £16.00 (2 adult + 3 child)
Group discounts are available if booked in advance.

Detailed Directions by Car:
From South: For Brechin Station, leave the A90 at the Brechin turn-off and go straight through the Town Centre. Pass the Northern Hotel, take the 2nd exit at the mini-roundabout then it is 150 yards to Park Road/St. Ninian Square; From North: For Brechin Station, leave the A90 at the Brechin turn-off and go straight through Trinity Village. Turn left at the mini-roundabout, it is then 250 yards to Park Road/St. Ninian Square. Bridge of Dun is situated half way between Brechin and Montrose. (Follow tourist signs).

CHASEWATER RAILWAY

Address: Chasewater Country Park,
Pool Road, Near Brownhills, Staffs,
WS8 7NL
Telephone Nº: (01543) 452623
Year Re-formed: 1985
Location of Line: Chasewater Country
Park, Brownhills, near Walsall
Length of Line: 2 miles

Nº of Steam Locos: 7
Nº of Other Locos: 8
Nº of Members: 380
Annual Membership Fee: Adult £7.50;
Family £12.50; Concessions £5.00
Approx Nº of Visitors P.A.: 18,000
Gauge: Standard

GENERAL INFORMATION

Nearest Mainline Station: Walsall or Birmingham
(both approximately 8 miles)
Nearest Bus Station: Walsall or Birmingham
Car Parking: Free parking in Chasewater Park
Coach Parking: Free parking in Chasewater Park
Souvenir Shop(s): Yes
Food & Drinks: Yes

SPECIAL INFORMATION

Chasewater Railway is based on the Cannock Chase
& Wolverhampton Railway opened in 1856. The
railway passed into the hands of the National Coal
Board which then ceased using the line in 1965.
An extension to Chasetown and a new station at
Chasewater Heaths is now open and a new heritage
centre is due to open during 2004.

OPERATING INFORMATION

Opening Times: Sundays and Bank Holidays
throughout the year and Saturdays from July to
September. Also some Santa Specials in December.
Steam Working: 11.30am, 12.50pm, 2.10pm,
3.30pm and 4.50pm.
Prices: Adult Return £2.45
            Child Return £2.45
            Family Return £6.45
All tickets offer unlimited rides on the day of issue.

Detailed Directions by Car:
Chasewater Country Park is situated in Brownhills off the A5 southbound near the junction of the A5 with the
A452 Chester Road. Follow the Brown tourist signs on the A5 for the Country Park.

CHINNOR & PRINCES RISBOROUGH RAILWAY

Address: Station Road, Chinnor, Oxon	**Nº of Steam Locos**: 1
Telephone Nº: (01844) 353535 (timetable)	**Nº of Other Locos**: 3
Year Formed: 1989	**Nº of Members**: 700
Location of Line: The Icknield Line, Chinnor	**Annual Membership Fee**: Adult £13.00; Family £20.00; Child £5.00; OAP £8.00
Length of Line: 3½ miles	**Approx Nº of Visitors P.A.**: 15,000
Gauge: Standard	**Web Site**: http://www.cprra.co.uk

GENERAL INFORMATION

Nearest Mainline Station: Princes Risborough (4 miles)
Nearest Bus Station: High Wycombe (10 miles)
Car Parking: Free parking at site
Coach Parking: Prior arrangement preferred but not necessary
Souvenir Shop(s): Yes
Food & Drinks: Soft drinks and light snacks in Station Buffet. Buffet usually available on trains.

SPECIAL INFORMATION

The Chinnor & Princes Risborough Railway operates the remaining 3½ mile section of the former GWR Watlington Branch from Chinnor to Thame Junction.

OPERATING INFORMATION

Opening Times: Most Saturdays and all Sundays from April to October + Santa Specials.
Steam Working: Operates from 10.00am to 5.00pm on Peak Season Sundays.
Prices: Adult Return £6.00
  Child Return £3.00
  Family Return £15.00
        (2 adults + 2 children)
  Senior Citizen Return £5.00

Detailed Directions by Car:
From All Parts: The railway at Chinnor is situated in Station Road just off the B4009. Junction 6 of the M40 is 4 miles away and Princes Risborough 4 miles further along the B4009. Once in Chinnor follow the brown Tourist signs to the railway.

CHOLSEY & WALLINGFORD RAILWAY

Address: P.O. Box 16, Hithercroft Road, Wallingford, Oxon OX10 9YN	**Nº of Steam Locos:** 1 (+ visiting Locos)
Telephone Nº: (01491) 835067 (24hr info)	**Nº of Other Locos:** 4
Year Formed: 1981	**Nº of Members:** 250
Location of Line: Wallingford, Oxon.	**Annual Membership Fee:** £10.00
Length of Line: 2½ miles	**Approx Nº of Visitors P.A.:** 4,000
	Gauge: Standard

GENERAL INFORMATION

Nearest Mainline Station: Joint station at Cholsey
Nearest Bus Station: Wallingford (¼ mile)
Car Parking: Roadside parking available
Coach Parking: Roadside parking available
Souvenir Shop(s): Yes
Food & Drinks: Yes

SPECIAL INFORMATION

The Wallingford branch was originally intended as a through line to Princes Risborough, via Watlington, but became the first standard gauge branch of Brunel's broad-gauge London to Bristol line.

OPERATING INFORMATION

Opening Times: Selected weekends from Easter until Christmas – phone for details.
Steam Working: Approximately 11.00am to 4.30pm
Prices: Adult Return £4.00
Child Return £3.00
Family Return £12.00 (2 adult + 2 child)
N.B. Prices are subject to change for Ivor the Engine events and Santa Specials.

Web site: www.cholsey-wallingford-railway.com

Detailed Directions by Car:
From All Parts: Exit from the A34 at the Milton Interchange (between E. Ilsley and Abingdon). Follow signs to Didcot and Wallingford. Take Wallingford bypass, then turn left at the first roundabout (signposted Hithercroft Estate). The Station is then ½ mile on the right.

CHURNET VALLEY RAILWAY

Address: The Railway Station, Cheddleton, Leek, Staffs. ST13 7EE
Telephone N°: (01538) 360522
Year Formed: 1978
Location of Line: Cheddleton to Froghall
Length of Line: 5½ miles

N° of Steam Locos: 2
N° of Other Locos: 3
N° of Members: –
Annual Membership Fee: £15.00
Approx N° of Visitors P.A.: 45,000
Gauge: Standard

GENERAL INFORMATION

Nearest Mainline Station: Stoke-on-Trent (12 miles)
Nearest Bus Station: Leek (5 miles)
Car Parking: Parking available on site
Coach Parking: Restricted space – please book in advance
Souvenir Shop(s): Yes
Food & Drinks: Yes

SPECIAL INFORMATION

Cheddleton Station is a Grade II listed building, Consall is a sleepy halt with Victorian charm, whereas Kingsley & Froghall are new NSR-style buildings.

OPERATING INFORMATION

Opening Times: Every Sunday from mid-March to mid-October. Saturdays in June, July and August and also Bank Holiday Mondays. A Diesel service runs from Tuesday to Thursday in June, July and August.
Steam Working: Please phone for a timetable.
Prices: Please telephone (01538) 360522 for details.

Detailed Directions by Car:
From All Parts: Take the M6 to Stoke-on-Trent and follow trunk roads to Leek. Cheddleton Station is just off the A520 Leek to Stone road. Kingsley & Froghall Station is just off the A52 Ashbourne Road.

CLEETHORPES COAST LIGHT RAILWAY

Address: King's Road, Cleethorpes,
North East Lincolnshire   DN35 0AG
Telephone Nº: (01472) 604657
Year Formed: 1948
Location of Line: Lakeside Park & Marine
embankment along Cleethorpes seafront
Length of Line: 1 mile

Nº of Steam Locos: 7
Nº of Other Locos: 4
Nº of Members: 65
Annual Membership Fee: Adult £11.00
Approx Nº of Visitors P.A.: 106,000
Gauge: 15 inches
Web: www.cleethorpescoastlightrailway.co.uk

GENERAL INFORMATION

Nearest Mainline Station: Cleethorpes (1 mile)
Nearest Bus Stop: Meridian Point (opposite)
Car Parking: Boating Lake car park – 500 spaces
(fee charged)
Coach Parking: As above
Souvenir Shop(s): Yes
Food & Drinks: Brief Encounters Tearoom on
Lakeside Station

SPECIAL INFORMATION

The Sutton Collection Museum opens in May 2004.

OPERATING INFORMATION

Opening Times: Open daily from 9th to 18th April
then daily from 1st May to 5th September. Open
during weekends, Bank holidays and school holidays
at all other times. Open 11.00am to dusk in Winter,
6.00pm in Summer.
Steam Working: Weekends throughout the year
Prices: Adult Return £2.20   (Single £1.80)
Child Return £1.80   (Single £1.40)
Family Return £7.00

Detailed Directions by Car:
Take the M180 to the A180 and continue to its' end. Follow signs for Cleethorpes. The Railway is situated along
Cleethorpes seafront 1 mile south of the Pier. Look for the brown Railway Engine tourist signs and the main
station is adjacent to the Leisure Centre.

COLNE VALLEY RAILWAY

Address: Castle Hedingham Station, Yeldham Road, Castle Hedingham, Essex, CO9 3DZ
Telephone Nº: (01787) 461174
Year Formed: 1974
Location of Line: On A1017, 7 miles north-west of Braintree
Length of Line: Approximately 1 mile

Nº of Steam Locos: 10
Nº of Other Locos: 11
Nº of Members: 280
Annual Membership Fee: £11.00
Approx Nº of Visitors P.A.: 45,000
Gauge: Standard
Web Site: www.colnevalleyrailway.co.uk

GENERAL INFORMATION

Nearest Mainline Station: Braintree (7 miles)
Nearest Bus Station: Hedingham bus from Braintree stops at the Railway (except on Sundays)
Car Parking: Parking at the site
Coach Parking: Free parking at site
Souvenir Shop(s): Yes
Food & Drinks: Yes – on operational days. Also Pullman Sunday Lunches – bookings necessary.

SPECIAL INFORMATION

The railway is being re-built on a section of the old Colne Valley & Halstead Railway, with all buildings, bridges, signal boxes, etc. re-located on site.
The Railway also has a Farm Park to visit on site (open between 3rd May and 21st September only).

OPERATING INFORMATION

Opening Times: Trains run every Sunday and Bank Holiday weekend from 14th March to the 24th October. Open daily from 31st July to 29th August. Pre-booked parties any time by arrangement.
Steam Working: Sundays 12.00pm to 4.00pm. Also Wednesdays & Thursdays in August 11.30am–3.30pm
Prices: Adult – Steam days £6; Diesel days £5.00; Static days £3.00
Child – Steam £3.00; Diesel £2.50; Static £1.50
Family (2 adults + 4 children) – Steam £18.00; Diesel £15.00; Static £7.50

Detailed Directions by Car:
The Railway is situated on the A1017 between Halstead and Haverhill, 7 miles north-west of Braintree.

CONWY VALLEY RAILWAY MUSEUM

Address: Old Goods Yard, Betws-y-Coed, Conwy, North Wales LL24 0AL	**Nº of Steam Locos**: 4
	Nº of Other Locos: 2
Telephone Nº: (01690) 710568	**Nº of Members**: –
Year Formed: 1983	**Annual Membership Fee**: –
Location of Line: Betws-y-Coed	**Approx Nº of Visitors P.A.**: 50,000
Length of Line: One and an eighth miles	**Gauge**: 7¼ inches and 15 inches

GENERAL INFORMATION

Nearest Mainline Station: Betws-y-Coed (20 yards)
Nearest Bus Station: 40 yards
Car Parking: Car park at site
Coach Parking: Car park at site
Souvenir Shop(s): Yes
Food & Drinks: Yes – Buffet Coach Cafe

SPECIAL INFORMATION

The Museum houses the unique 3D dioramas by the late Jack Nelson. Also the ¼ size steam loco 'Britannia'.

OPERATING INFORMATION

Opening Times: Daily from March to the end of October 10.15am to 5.00pm. Open daily in the Winter from 10.15am to 4.00pm.
Trains Working: Daily from 10.15am
Prices: Adult – £1 entry to museum; Train £1.00; Tram 80p
Child/OAP – 50p entry to museum; Train £1.00; Tram 80p
Family tickets – £2.50

Detailed Directions by Car:
From Midlands & South: Take M54/M6 onto the A5 and into Betws-y-Coed; From Other Parts: Take the A55 coast road then the A470 to Betws-y-Coed. The museum is located by the Mainline Station directly off the A5.

DARLINGTON RAILWAY CENTRE & MUSEUM

Address: North Road Station, Darlington, Co. Durham DL3 6ST
Telephone N°: (01325) 460532
Year Formed: 1975
Location of Line: Adjacent to North Road Station
Length of Line: ¼ mile

N° of Steam Locos: 5
N° of Other Locos: –
N° of Members: –
Annual Membership Fee: –
Approx N° of Visitors P.A.: 32,000
Gauge: Standard
Web site: www.drcm.org.uk

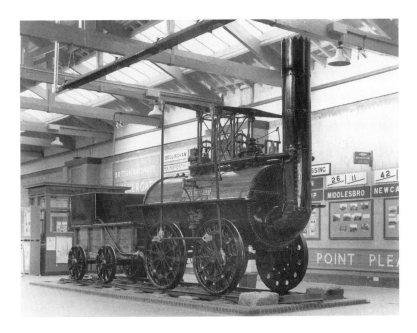

GENERAL INFORMATION

Nearest Mainline Station: North Road (adjacent)
Nearest Bus Station: Darlington (1 mile)
Car Parking: Free parking at site
Coach Parking: Free parking at site
Souvenir Shop(s): Yes
Food & Drinks: Cafe at weekends in the Summer, drinks machine and confectionery at other times.

SPECIAL INFORMATION

The museum is an 1842 station on the route of the Stockton and Darlington Railway and is devoted to the Railways of north-east England.

OPERATING INFORMATION

Opening Times: The Museum is open 10.00am to 5.00pm daily except Christmas Day, Boxing Day and New Year's Day.
The Locomotive Works run by the A1 Steam Locomotive Trust is open on the 2nd Saturday of each month.
Prices: Adult – £2.20
Child – £1.10

Detailed Directions by Car:
From Darlington Town Centre: Follow the A167 north for about ¾ mile then turn left immediately before the Railway bridge; From A1(M): Exit at Junction 59 then follow A167 towards Darlington and turn right after passing under the Railway bridge.

DEAN FOREST RAILWAY

Address: Norchard Centre, Forest Road; Lydney, Gloucestershire GL15 4ET	**Nº of Steam Locos**: 7 (2 working)
Telephone Nº: (01594) 845840	**Nº of Other Locos**: 18
Information Line: (01594) 843423 (24 hr.)	**Nº of Members**: 880
Year Formed: 1970	**Annual Membership Fee**: Adult £13.00; Family (4 persons) £16.00
Location of Line: Lydney, Gloucestershire	**Approx Nº of Visitors P.A.**: 55,000
Length of Line: 3¼ miles	**Gauge**: Standard

GENERAL INFORMATION

Nearest Mainline Station: Lydney (200 metres)
Nearest Bus Station: Lydney (1 mile)
Car Parking: 600 spaces available at Norchard
Coach Parking: Ample space available
Souvenir Shop(s): Yes + a Museum
Food & Drinks: Yes – on operational days only

SPECIAL INFORMATION

Dean Forest Railway preserves the sole surviving line of the Severn and Wye Railway. The Railway is lengthening the line to a total of 4¼ miles. The section north of Norchard to Whitecroft is now worked by DMU from Norchard giving a round trip of 6½ miles.

OPERATING INFORMATION

Opening Times: Norchard is open every day for viewing. Trains operate from 21st March to 31st October and also on selected days from 5th to 24th December. Special events also run on various days throughout the year – phone the Railway for details.
Steam Working: Trains depart Norchard at 11.25am, 12.30pm, 1.25pm, 2.30pm and 3.25pm.
Prices: Adult Return £6.50
Child Return £4.50 (ages 5-16 years old)
Senior Citizens £5.50
N.B. Fares may differ on special dates.

Web site: www.deanforestrailway.co.uk

Detailed Directions by Car:
From M50 & Ross-on-Wye: Take the B4228 and B4234 via Coleford to reach Lydney. Norchard is located on the B4234, ¾ mile north of Lydney Town Centre; From Monmouth: Take the A4136 and B4431 onto the B4234 via Coleford; From South Wales: Take the M4 then M48 onto the A48 via Chepstow to Lydney; From Midlands/Gloucester: Take the M5 to Gloucester then the A48 to Lydney; From the West Country: Take the M4 and M48 via the 'Old' Severn Bridge to Chepstow and then the A48 to Lydney.

DERWENT VALLEY LIGHT RAILWAY

Address: Murton Park, Murton Lane, Murton, York YO19 5UF	**No of Steam Locos**: 2
Telephone No: (01904) 489966	**No of Other Locos**: 5
Year Formed: 1991	**No of Members**: 200
Location of Line: Murton, near York	**Annual Membership Fee**: £8.00
Length of Line: ½ mile	**Approx No of Visitors P.A.**: 10,000
	Gauge: Standard

GENERAL INFORMATION

Nearest Mainline Station: York (4 miles)
Nearest Bus Station: York (4 miles)
Car Parking: Large free car park at the site
Coach Parking: Free at the site
Souvenir Shop(s): Yes – at the Yorkshire Museum of Farming (same site)
Food & Drinks: Yes – as above

SPECIAL INFORMATION

The site is the remnants of the Derwent Valley Railway which was the last privately owned railway in England, originally opened in 1913.

OPERATING INFORMATION

Opening Times: Sundays and Bank Holidays from Easter until the end of September. Also Santa Specials run in December.
Steam Working: Last Sunday in the month and Bank Holidays – 10.00am to 5.00pm.
Prices: Adult £4.50
Child £2.50
Senior Citizens £3.50
Family Tickets £12.00 (2 adult + 4 child)
Prices are for entrance to the Yorkshire Museum of Farming – train rides are included in the price.

Detailed Directions by Car:
From All Parts: The railway is well signposted for the Yorkshire Museum of Farming from the A64 (York to Scarborough road), the A1079 (York to Hull road) and the A166 (York to Bridlington road).

DIDCOT RAILWAY CENTRE

Address: Didcot Railway Centre, Didcot, Oxfordshire OX11 7NJ	**Nº of Steam Locos**: 23
Telephone Nº: (01235) 817200	**Nº of Other Locos**: 2
Year Formed: 1961	**Nº of Members**: 4,400
Location of Line: Didcot	**Annual Membership Fee**: Full £24.00; Over 60/Under 18 £16.00; Family £30.00
Length of Line: ¾ mile	**Approx Nº of Visitors P.A.**: 70,000
Gauge: Standard	**Web Site**: www.didcotrailwaycentre.org.uk

GENERAL INFORMATION

Nearest Mainline Station: Didcot Parkway (adjacent)
Nearest Bus Station: Buses to Didcot call at the Railway station
Car Parking: BR car park adjacent
Coach Parking: Further details on application
Souvenir Shop(s): Yes
Food & Drinks: Yes

SPECIAL INFORMATION

The Centre is based on a Great Western Railway engine shed and is devoted to the re-creation of part of the GWR.

OPERATING INFORMATION

Opening Times: Weekends all year round, open daily from 29th May to 5th September. Weekends and Steam days open 10.00am to 5.00pm. Other days and during Winter open 10.00am to 4.00pm.
Steam Working: First and last Sundays of each month. Bank Holidays, all Sundays July and August, all Wednesdays 14th July to 1st September. Also on Saturdays in August.
Prices: Adult £4.00 – £8.00 (including rides)
Child £3.00 – £6.50 (including rides)
Discounted family tickets are often available (2 adults + 2 children).
Prices vary depending on the events.

Detailed Directions by Car:
From East & West: Take the M4 to Junction 13 then the A34 and A4130 (follow brown Tourist signs to Didcot Railway Centre); From North: The centre is signed from the A34 to A4130.

DOBWALLS FAMILY ADVENTURE PARK

Address: Dobwalls Family Adventure Park, near Liskeard, Cornwall PL14 6HB
Telephone Nº: (01579) 320325/321129
Year Formed: 1970
Location of Line: Near Liskeard, Cornwall
Length of Line: 2 × 1 mile tracks

Nº of Steam Locos: 6
Nº of Other Locos: 4
Nº of Members: –
Annual Membership Fee: –
Gauge: 7¼ inches
Web site: www.dobwallsadventurepark.co.uk

GENERAL INFORMATION

Nearest Mainline Station: Liskeard (3 miles)
Nearest Bus Station: Most National Express Coaches travel through Dobwalls.
Car Parking: Ample parking available at site
Coach Parking: Large coach park available
Souvenir Shop(s): Yes
Food & Drinks: Yes

SPECIAL INFORMATION

Formerly known as the Forest Railroad Park, Dobwalls has a large number of other attractions including many for children. There is also an art gallery.

OPERATING INFORMATION

Opening Times: Open most days from Easter until the end of October. Opens from 10.30am to 5.00pm.
Steam Working: All days when open
Prices: Children under the age of 2 – Free
Single person ticket – £8.95
Family ticket (2 people) – £17.50
Family ticket (3 people) – £26.00
Family ticket (4 people) – £34.00
Family ticket (5 people) – £42.50
Family ticket (6 people) – £51.00
Disabled & Senior Citizens – £5.50
SuperSaver (weekends after 2.00pm) – £5.00
Group Price (20 people or more) – £5.50 per person

Detailed Directions by Car:
From All Parts: Dobwalls Family Adventure Park is situated just off the A38 at Dobwalls village, 3 miles from Liskeard.

DOWNPATRICK RAILWAY MUSEUM

Address: Market Street, Downpatrick, Co. Down, Northern Ireland	**Nº of Steam Locos**: 3
Telephone Nº: (028) 4461-5779	**Nº of Other Locos**: 5
Year Formed: 1985	**Nº of Members**: 180
Location of Line: Downpatrick	**Annual Membership Fee**: Adult £15.00, Family £20.00, Concessions £10.00
Length of Line: 1 mile	**Approx Nº of Visitors P.A.**: 13,000
Gauge: Standard	**Web**: www.downpatricksteamrailway.co.uk

GENERAL INFORMATION

Nearest Mainline Station: –
Nearest Bus Station: Adjacent to Station
Car Parking: Ample parking adjacent to Station
Coach Parking: Ample parking adjacent to Station
Souvenir Shop(s): Yes
Food & Drinks: Yes

SPECIAL INFORMATION

This is the only operating Standard (5' 3") Gauge Heritage Railway in Ireland.

OPERATING INFORMATION

Opening Times: The Museum is open daily from June to September.
Steam Working: Saturdays and Sundays in July, August and also first 2 Sundays in September. Trains are usually steam hauled and run from 2.00pm to 5.00pm. Special trains run at Easter, Halloween and Christmas.
Prices: Adult £3.80
          Child £2.80

Detailed Directions by Car:
From Belfast take the A7 Downpatrick Road. Upon arrival in Downpatrick, follow the brown tourist signs and the Railway Museum is adjacent to the bus station.

EAST ANGLIAN RAILWAY MUSEUM

Address: Chappel & Wakes Colne Station, Colchester, Essex CO6 2DS	**No of Steam Locos:** 8 **Other Locos:** 4
Telephone No: (01206) 242524	**No of Members:** 750
Year Formed: 1969	**Annual Membership Fee:** Adult £20.00; Senior Citizen £15.00
Location of Line: 6 miles west of Colchester on Marks Tey to Sudbury branch	**Approx No of Visitors P.A.:** 40,000
Length of Line: A third of a mile	**Gauge:** Standard
	Web site: www.earm.co.uk

GENERAL INFORMATION

Nearest Mainline Station: Chappel & Wakes Colne (adajcent)
Nearest Bus Stop: Chappel (400 yards)
Car Parking: Free parking at site
Coach Parking: Free parking at site
Souvenir Shop(s): Yes
Food & Drinks: Yes – drinks are available every day and snacks are also available on operating days.

SPECIAL INFORMATION

The museum has the most comprehensive collection of railway architecture & engineering in the region.

OPERATING INFORMATION

Opening Times: Open daily 10.00am to 5.00pm. Steam days open from 11.00am to 5.00pm
Steam Working: Steam days are held every month from April to August and also in October and December. Bank Holidays are also Steam days.
Prices: Adult £3.00 non-Steam; £6.00 Steam
          Child £2.00 non-Steam; £3.00 Steam
          O.A.P. £2.50 non-Steam; £4.50 Steam
          Family £8.00 non-Steam; £15.00 Steam
Children under the age of 4 are admitted free of charge. A 10% discount is available for bookings for more than 10 people.

Detailed Directions by Car:
From North & South: Turn off the A12 south west of Colchester onto the A1124 (formerly the A604). The Museum is situated just off the A1124; From West: Turn off the A120 just before Marks Tey (signposted).

EASTBOURNE MINIATURE STEAM RAILWAY

Address: Lottbridge Drove, Eastbourne, East Sussex   BN23 6NS
Telephone Nº: (01323) 520229
Year Formed: 1992
Location of Line: Eastbourne
Length of Line: 1 mile

Nº of Steam Locos: 5
Nº of Other Locos: 2
Nº of Members: –
Approx Nº of Visitors P.A.: –
Gauge: 7¼ inches
Web site: www.emsr.co.uk

GENERAL INFORMATION

Nearest Mainline Station: Eastbourne (2 miles)
Nearest Bus Station: Eastbourne (2 miles)
Car Parking: Free parking on site
Coach Parking: Free parking on site
Souvenir Shop(s): Yes
Food & Drinks: Yes

SPECIAL INFORMATION

The Railway site also has many other attractions including model railways, an adventure playground, nature walk, maze, picnic area, Cafe and day-ticket Angling.

OPERATING INFORMATION

Opening Times: Open 10.00am to 5.00pm daily from the weekend before Easter to the end of September. Also special events on Easter Sunday.
Steam Working: Weekends, Bank Holidays and during School Holidays. Diesel at other times.
Prices: Adult £3.95
              Child £3.45 (2 years and under free)
              Family Tickets £14.00
                                (2 adults + 2 children)

Detailed Directions by Car:
From All Parts: Take the A22 new road to Eastbourne then follow the Brown tourist signs for the 'Mini Railway'.

EAST KENT RAILWAY

Address: Station Road, Shepherdswell, Dover, Kent CT15 7PD **Telephone Nº:** (01304) 832042 **Year Formed:** 1985 **Location of Line:** Between Shepherdswell and Eythorne **Length of Line:** 2 miles	**Nº of Steam Locos:** 2 **Nº of Other Locos:** 5 **Nº of Members:** 400 **Annual Membership Fee:** £15.00 (Adult) **Approx Nº of Visitors P.A.:** 15,000 **Gauge:** Standard and also 5 inch and 3¼ inch miniature guage

GENERAL INFORMATION

Nearest Mainline Station: Shepherdswell (50 yards)
Car Parking: Available Shepherdswell and Eythorne
Coach Parking: In adjacent Station Yard
Souvenir Shop(s): Yes
Food & Drinks: Yes

SPECIAL INFORMATION

The East Kent Railway was originally built between 1911 and 1917 to service Tilmanstone Colliery. Closed in the mid-1980's, the railway was re-opened in 1995.

OPERATING INFORMATION

Opening Times: Open weekends throughout the year for static viewing from 11.00am to 3.00pm. Trains run during Easter and Sundays from May to September and also weekends in December.
Steam Working: During special events only. Please contact the railway for details.
Prices: Adult £5.00
Child £3.50
Senior Citizens £4.00

Web site: www.eastkentrailway.com

Detailed Directions by Car:
From the A2: Take the turning to Shepherdswell and continue to the village. Pass the shop on the left and cross the railway bridge. Take the next left (Station Road) signposted at the traffic lights for the EKR; From the A256: Take the turning for Eythorne at the roundabout on the section between Eastry and Whitfield. Follow the road through Eythorne. Further on you will cross the railway line and enter Shepherdswell. After a few hundred yards take the right turn signposted for the EKR.

EAST LANCASHIRE RAILWAY

Address: Bolton Street Station, Bury, Lancashire BL9 0EY	**Nº of Steam Locos**: 14
Telephone Nº: (0161) 764-7790	**Nº of Other Locos**: 16
Year Formed: 1968	**Nº of Members**: 4,500
Location of Line: Heywood, Bury and Rawtenstall	**Annual Membership Fee**: £14.00
Length of Line: 12 miles	**Approx Nº of Visitors P.A.**: 110,000
	Gauge: Standard

GENERAL INFORMATION

Nearest Mainline Station: Manchester (then Metro Link to Bury)
Nearest Bus Station: ¼ mile
Car Parking: Adjacent
Coach Parking: Adjacent
Souvenir Shop(s): Yes
Food & Drinks: Yes

SPECIAL INFORMATION

Originally opened in 1846, the East Lancashire Railway was re-opened in 1991.

OPERATING INFORMATION

Opening Times: Every weekend & Bank Holiday 9.00am to 5.00pm. Also Wednesday to Friday from May to September inclusive.
Steam Working: Most trains are steam-hauled. Saturdays alternate Steam & Diesel. 2 engines in steam on Sundays.
Prices: Adult Return £9.50
Child Return £6.50
Family Return £24.00
Cheaper fares are available for shorter journeys.

Detailed Directions by Car:
From All Parts: Exit the M66 at Junction 2 and take the A56 into Bury. Follow the brown tourist signs and turn right into Bolton Street at the junction with the A58. The station is about 150 yards on the right.

EASTLEIGH LAKESIDE RAILWAY

Address: Lakeside Country Park, Wide Lane, Eastleigh, Hants. SO50 5PE	**Nº of Steam Locos:** 12
Telephone Nº: (023) 8061-2020	**Nº of Other Locos:** 4
Year Formed: 1992	**Nº of Members:** –
Location: Opposite Southampton airport	**Approx Nº of Visitors P.A.:** 60,000
Length of Line: 1¼ miles	**Gauge:** 10¼ inches and 7¼ inches
	Web site: www.steamtrain.co.uk

GENERAL INFORMATION

Nearest Mainline Station: Southampton Airport (Parkway) (¼ mile)
Nearest Bus Station: Eastleigh (1½ miles)
Car Parking: Free parking available on site
Coach Parking: Free parking available on site
Souvenir Shop(s): Yes
Food & Drinks: Yes

SPECIAL INFORMATION

The railway also has a playground and picnic area overlooking the lakes.

OPERATING INFORMATION

Opening Times: Weekends throughout the year and daily during July, August and September plus all school holidays. Open 10.30am to 4.30pm.
Santa Specials run on some dates in December.
Steam Working: As above
Prices: Standard Class Single £1.30; Return £2.00
First Class Single £1.50; Return £2.50
3 rides per person – Standard £4.00; First £5.00
Annual season tickets are available. Children under the age of 2 years ride free of charge.

Detailed Directions by Car:
From All Parts: Exit the M27 at Junction 5 and take the A335 to Eastleigh. The Railway is situated 1¼ miles past Southampton Airport Station.

EAST SOMERSET RAILWAY (STRAWBERRY LINE)

Address: Cranmore Railway Station, Shepton Mallet, Somerset BA4 4QP
Telephone No: (01749) 880417
Year Formed: 1971
Location of Line: Cranmore, off A361 between Frome and Shepton Mallet
Length of Line: 3 miles

No of Steam Locos: 5
No of Other Locos: 2
No of Members: 480
Annual Membership Fee: Single £13.00; Couple £17.00; Family £25.00
Approx No of Visitors P.A.: 20,000
Gauge: Standard

GENERAL INFORMATION

Nearest Mainline Station: Castle Cary (10 miles)
Nearest Bus Station: Shepton Mallet (3 miles)
Car Parking: Space for 100 cars available
Coach Parking: Available by arrangement
Souvenir Shop(s): Yes
Food & Drinks: Yes

SPECIAL INFORMATION

Footplate experience courses available – phone (01749) 880417 for further details.

Web site: www.eastsomersetrailway.com

OPERATING INFORMATION

Opening Times: Complex, Museum and Engine Sheds open daily except for 24th & 25th December.
Steam Working: Sundays in the Winter, weekends and bank holidays in April, May & October plus some weekdays in the Summer. Santa Specials run on weekends in December. Other special events run on various dates. Open 10.00am to 4.00pm in the Winter, 10.00am to 5.30pm in the Summer.
Prices: Adult £6.00
  Child £4.00
  Senior Citizens £5.00
  Family £17.00

Detailed Directions by Car:
From the North: Take A367/A37 to Shepton Mallet then turn left onto A361 to Frome. Carry on to Shepton Mallet and 9 miles after Frome turn left at Cranmore; From the South: Take A36 to Frome bypass then A361 to Cranmore; From the West: Take A371 from Wells to Shepton Mallet, then A361 to Frome (then as above).

ELSECAR STEAM RAILWAY

Address: Wath Road, Elsecar, Barnsley, S74 8HJ	**Nº of Steam Locos:** 2
	Nº of Other Locos: 2
Telephone Nº: (01226) 740203	**Nº of Members:** –
Year Formed: –	**Annual Membership Fee:** –
Location of Line: Elsecar, near Barnsley	**Approx Nº of Visitors P.A.:** –
Length of Line: 1 mile	**Gauge:** Standard
	Web site: www.barnsley.gov.uk

GENERAL INFORMATION

Nearest Mainline Station: Elsecar
Nearest Bus Station: Barnsley
Car Parking: Large free car park at the site
Coach Parking: At the site
Souvenir Shop(s): Yes
Food & Drinks: Yes

SPECIAL INFORMATION

The Railway is based at the Elsecar Heritage Centre which is an antiques and craft centre with a wide range of displays and special events.

OPERATING INFORMATION

Opening Times: Daily from 10.00am to 5.00pm throughout the year except from 25th December to 2nd January.
Steam Working: Sundays from March to October – hourly from 12.00pm to 4.00pm and on special event days. Please phone for details.
Prices: Adult £2.50
　　　　　Senior Citizens/Under 13's £1.00
Admission to the museum and site is free of charge except for the Living History Centre and during Special Events.

Detailed Directions by Car:
From All Parts: Exit the M1 at Junction 36 and follow the brown 'Elsecar Heritage' signs taking the A6135 for approximately 2 miles. Turn left onto Broad Carr Road for just under a mile, then right onto Armroyd Lane and right again onto Fitzwilliam Street. Free visitor car parking is available on Wentworth Road off the junction of Fitzwilliam Street and Wath Road.

EMBSAY & BOLTON ABBEY STEAM RAILWAY

Address: Bolton Abbey Station, Bolton Abbey, Skipton, N. Yorkshire BD23 6AF	**N° of Steam Locos**: 21
Telephone N°: (01756) 710614	**N° of Other Locos**: 11
Year Formed: 1968	**N° of Members**: 700
Location of Line: 2 miles east of Skipton	**Annual Membership Fee**: £10.00
Length of Line: 4½ miles	**Approx N° of Visitors P.A.**: 107,000
	Gauge: Standard

GENERAL INFORMATION

Nearest Mainline Station: Skipton (2 miles), Ilkley (3 miles)

Nearest Bus Station: Skipton (2 miles), Ilkley (3 mls)

Car Parking: Large car park at both Stations

Coach Parking: Large coach park at both Stations

Souvenir Shop(s): Yes

Food & Drinks: Yes – Cafe + Buffet cars

SPECIAL INFORMATION

The line extension to Bolton Abbey opened in 1998.

Web site: www.embsayboltonabbeyrailway.org.uk

OPERATING INFORMATION

Opening Times: Every Sunday throughout the year. Weekends from April to the end of October and daily in the summer season.

Steam Working: Trains depart Embsay Station at 10.30am, 12.00pm, 1.30pm, 3.00pm and 4.30pm during the Main Season. Mondays and Wednesdays are operated by a D.M.U.

Prices: Adult Return £6.00
Child Return £3.00
Family Ticket £16.00 (2 adult + 2 children)

Different fares may apply on special event days.

Detailed Directions by Car:

From All Parts: Embsay Station is off the A59 Skipton bypass by the Harrogate Road. Bolton Abbey Station is off the A59 at Bolton Abbey.

EVESHAM VALE LIGHT RAILWAY

Address: Evesham Country Park, Twyford, Evesham WR11 4TP	**Nº of Steam Locos:** 4
Telephone Nº: (01386) 422282	**Nº of Other Locos:** 3
Year Formed: 2002	**Nº of Members:** None
Location of Line: 1 mile north of Evesham	**Approx Nº of Visitors P.A.:** 40,000
Length of Line: 1¼ miles	**Gauge:** 15 inches
	Web site: www.evlr.co.uk

GENERAL INFORMATION

Nearest Mainline Station: Evesham (1 mile)
Nearest Bus Station: Evesham (1½ miles)
Car Parking: Available in the Country Park
Coach Parking: Available in the Country Park
Souvenir Shop(s): Yes
Food & Drinks: Restaurant at the Garden Centre

SPECIAL INFORMATION

The railway is situated within the 130 acre Evesham Country Park which has apple orchards and picnic areas overlooking the picturesque Vale of Evesham.

OPERATING INFORMATION

Opening Times: Open at weekends throughout the year and daily during school holidays. Trains run from 10.30am to 5.00pm. The 2004 Gala event runs on 3rd and 4th July. Please phone for further details.
Steam Working: Daily when trains are running
Prices: Adult Return £1.50
Child Return £1.00
Senior Citizen Return £1.30

Detailed Directions by Car:
From the North: Exit the M42 at Junction 3 and take the A435 towards Alcester then the A46 to Evesham; From the South: Exit the M5 at Junction 9 and take the A46 to Evesham; From the West: Exit the M5 at Junction 7 and take the A44 to Evesham; From the East: Take the A44 from Oxford to Evesham. Upon reaching Evesham, follow the Brown tourist signs for Evesham Country Park and the railway.

EXBURY GARDENS RAILWAY

Address: Exbury Gardens, Exbury, Near Southampton SO45 1AZ	**Nº of Steam Locos:** 2
Telephone Nº: (02380) 891203	**Nº of Other Locos:** 1
Year Formed: 2001	**Nº of Members:** None
Location of Line: Exbury	**Approx Nº of Visitors P.A.:** 55,000
Length of Line: 1½ miles	**Gauge:** 12¼ inches
	Web site: www.exbury.co.uk

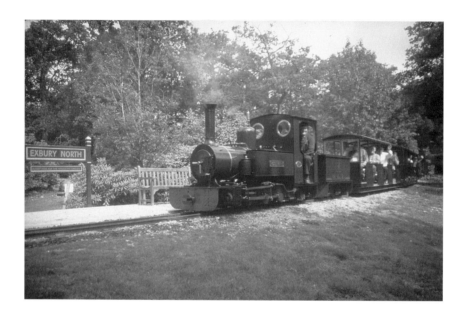

GENERAL INFORMATION

Nearest Mainline Station: Brockenhurst (8 miles)
Nearest Bus Station: Southampton (12 miles)
Car Parking: Available on site
Coach Parking: Available on site
Souvenir Shop(s): Yes
Food & Drinks: Available

SPECIAL INFORMATION

The railway is located in the world famous Azalea and Rhododendron gardens at Exbury.

OPERATING INFORMATION

Opening Times: Daily from the 28th February to 31st October. Also during weekends in December. Open from 11.00am to 5.00pm.
Steam Working: Every running day.
Prices: Adult Return £2.00 – £3.00
Child Return £2.00 – £3.00

Detailed Directions by Car:
Exit the M27 at Junction 2 and take the A326 to Dibden. Follow signs for Exbury.

FAIRBOURNE & BARMOUTH RAILWAY

Address: Beach Road, Fairbourne, Dolgellau, Gwynedd LL38 2EX
Telephone Nº: (01341) 250362
Year Formed: 1947
Location of Line: On A493 between Tywyn & Dolgellau
Length of Line: 2¼ miles

Nº of Steam Locos: 4
Nº of Other Locos: 2
Nº of Members: 87
Annual Membership Fee: £8.00
Approx Nº of Visitors P.A.: 25,000
Gauge: 12¼ inches
Web Site: www.fairbournerailway.com

GENERAL INFORMATION

Nearest Mainline Station: Fairbourne (adjacent)
Nearest Bus Station: Fairbourne (adjacent)
Car Parking: Available in Mainline station car park
Coach Parking: Pay & Display car park 300 yards (the Railway will re-imburse car parking charges for party bookings)
Souvenir Shop(s): Yes
Food & Drinks: Yes – Tea room at Fairbourne, Cafe at Porth Penrhyn Terminus

SPECIAL INFORMATION

There is a connecting ferry service (passenger only) to Barmouth from Porth Penrhyn Terminus.

OPERATING INFORMATION

Opening Times: Open daily from 8th to 18th April and from 1st May to 21st September. Also opens from 23rd October to 31st October. Santa Specials run on 11th and 12th December at 1.30pm.
Steam Working: 11.00am to 3.45pm for normal service. At peak times 10.40am to 4.20pm.
Prices: Adult Return £6.40
Child Return £3.60
Family £16.05 (2 adults + up to 3 children)
Senior Citizen Return £5.40

Detailed Directions by Car:
From North & East Wales: Follow Dolgellau signs, turn left onto A493 towards Tywyn. The turn-off for Fairbourne is located 9 miles south west of Dolgellau; From South Wales: Follow signs for Machynlleth, then follow A487 towards Dolgellau. Then take A493 towards Fairbourne.

FFESTINIOG RAILWAY

Address: Ffestiniog Railway, Harbour Station, Porthmadog, Gwynedd LL49 9NF **Telephone Nº**: (01766) 516073 **Year Formed**: 1832 **Location of Line**: Porthmadog to Blaenau Ffestiniog **Length of Line**: 13½ miles	**Nº of Steam Locos**: 12 **Nº of Other Locos**: 12 **Nº of Members**: 5,000 **Annual Membership Fee**: £18.00 **Approx Nº of Visitors P.A.**: 200,000 **Gauge**: 1 foot 11½ inches **Web Site**: www.festrail.co.uk

GENERAL INFORMATION

Nearest Mainline Station: Blaenau Ffestiniog (interchange)
Nearest Bus Station: Bus stop next to stations at Porthmadog & Blaenau Ffestiniog
Car Parking: Parking available at Porthmadog, Blaenau Ffestiniog and Minffordd
Coach Parking: Available at Porthmadog and Blaenau Ffestiniog
Souvenir Shop(s): Yes
Food & Drinks: Yes

SPECIAL INFORMATION

The Railway runs through the spectacular scenery of Snowdonia National Park.

OPERATING INFORMATION

Opening Times: Daily service from the 27th March to 31st October. Limited service in the Winter. Train times vary.
Steam Working: Most trains are steam hauled. Limited in the Winter, however.
Prices: Adult £14.00 (All-day Rover ticket)
Child £7.00 (1 child free with each adult)
Reductions are available for Senior Citizens, Families and groups of 20 or more.

Detailed Directions by Car:
Portmadog is easily accessible from the Midlands – take the M54/A5 to Corwen then the A494 to Bala onto the A4212 to Trawsfynydd and the A470 (becomes the A487 from Maentwrog) to Porthmadog. From Chester take the A55 to Llandudno Junction and the A470 to Blaenau Ffestiniog. Both Stations are well-signposted.

FOXFIELD STEAM RAILWAY

Address: Caverswall Road Station, Blythe Bridge, Stoke-on-Trent, Staffs. ST11 9EA	**No of Steam Locos:** 16
Telephone No: (01782) 396210	**No of Other Locos:** 15
Year Formed: 1967	**No of Members:** Over 300
Location of Line: Blythe Bridge	**Annual Membership Fee:** Adult £8.00; Junior £5.00; Family £12.00
Length of Line: 3½ miles	**Approx No of Visitors P.A.:** 25,000
Gauge: Standard	**Web site:** www.foxfieldrailway.co.uk

GENERAL INFORMATION

Nearest Mainline Station: Blythe Bridge (¼ mile)
Nearest Bus Station: Hanley (5 miles)
Car Parking: Space for 300 cars available
Coach Parking: Space for 6 coaches available
Souvenir Shop(s): Yes
Food & Drinks: Yes – Buffet and Real Ale Bar

SPECIAL INFORMATION

The Railway is a former Colliery railway built in 1893 to take coal from Foxfield Colliery. It has the steepest Standard Gauge adhesion worked gradient in the UK.

OPERATING INFORMATION

Opening Times: Sundays & Bank Holiday Mondays from 21st March to the end of October. Also weekends in December. Open 10.30am to 5.00pm.
Steam Working: 11.30am, 1.00pm, 2.00pm. 3.00pm & 4.00pm
Prices: Adult Tickets – £5.00
Child Tickets – £3.50
Senior Citizen Tickets – £4.50
Family Tickets – £14.00
Fares may vary on special event days.

Detailed Directions by Car:
From South: Exit M6 at Junction 14 onto the A34 to Stone then the A520 to Meir and the A50 to Blythe Bridge; From North: Exit M6 at Junction 15 then the A500 to Stoke-on-Trent and the A50 to Blythe Bridge; From East: Take the A50 to Blythe Bridge. Once in Blythe Bridge, turn by the Mainline crossing.

GIANT'S CAUSEWAY & BUSHMILLS RAILWAY

Address: Giant's Causeway Station, Runkerry Road, Bushmills, Co. Antrim, Northern Ireland BT57 8SZ
Telephone Nº: (028) 2073-2844
Information Line: (028) 2073-2594
Year Formed: 2002
Location: Between the distillery village of Bushmills and the Giant's Causeway

Length of Line: 2 miles
Nº of Steam Locos: 2
Nº of Other Locos: 1
Nº of Members: None
Approx Nº of Visitors P.A.: 50,000
Gauge: 3 feet
Web site: www.giantscausewayrailway.org

GENERAL INFORMATION

Nearest Northern Ireland Railway Station: Coleraine/Portrush
Nearest Bus Station: Coleraine/Portrush
Car Parking: Free parking available on site. By parking at the Bushmills Station and taking the railway expensive parking charges at the Causeway itself can be avoided.
Coach Parking: Available on site
Souvenir Shop(s): Yes
Food & Drinks: At Giant's Causeway Station only

SPECIAL INFORMATION

The railway links the distillery village of Bushmills (open to visitors) to the World Heritage Site of the Giant's Causeway. The railway itself is built on the final two miles of the pioneering hydro-electric tramway which linked the Giant's Causeway to the main railway at Portrush from 1883 to 1949.

OPERATING INFORMATION

Opening Times: Usually daily from mid-May to the end of September and for two weeks over Easter. Also open at weekends from Easter until mid-May and during October. Trains run from 11.00am.
Steam Working: Usually daily. Please ring the Information Line shown above for more details.
Prices: Adult Return £5.00
Adult Single £3.50
Child Return £3.00
Child Single £2.00
Note: Family Tickets are also available

Detailed Directions by Car:
From Belfast take the M2 to the junction with the A26 (for Antrim, Ballymena and Coleraine). Follow the A26/M2/A26. From Ballymoney onwards Bushmills and the Giant's Causeway are well signposted. The railway is also well signposted in the immediate vicinity.

GLOUCESTERSHIRE WARWICKSHIRE RAILWAY

Address: The Station, Toddington,
Cheltenham, Gloucestershire   GL54 5DT
Telephone Nº: (01242) 621405
Year Formed: 1981
Location of Line: 5 miles south of
Broadway, Worcestershire, near the A46
Length of Line: 10 miles

Nº of Steam Locos: 11
Nº of Other Locos: 17
Nº of Members: 2,650
Annual Membership Fee: £11.00 (Adult)
Approx Nº of Visitors P.A.: 50,000
Gauge: Standard gauge
Web site: www.gwsr.plc.uk

GENERAL INFORMATION

Nearest Mainline Station: Cheltenham Spa or
Ashchurch
Nearest Bus Station: Cheltenham
Car Parking: Parking available at Toddington,
Winchcombe & Cheltenham Racecourse Stations
Coach Parking: Parking available as above
Souvenir Shop(s): Yes
Food & Drinks: Yes

SPECIAL INFORMATION

A narrow gauge railway is adjacent.

OPERATING INFORMATION

Opening Times: Sundays in November. Weekends
& Bank Holidays during the rest of the year. Also
daily during School Holidays. 10.00am to 5.00pm
Steam Working: Most operating days
Prices: Adult Return £9.00
Child Return £5.50
Senior Citizen Return £7.50
Family Return £24.00 (2 Adult + 3 Child)
Under 5's free of charge

Detailed Directions by Car:
Toddington is 11 miles north east of Cheltenham, 5 miles south of Broadway just off the B4632 (old A46). Exit the
M5 at Junction 9 towards Stow-on-the-Wold for the B4632. The Railway is clearly visible from the B4632.

GREAT CENTRAL RAILWAY

Address: Great Central Station, Great
Central Road, Loughborough,
Leicestershire LE11 1RW
Telephone Nº: (01509) 230726
Year Formed: 1969
Location of Line: From Loughborough
to Leicester

Length of Line: 8 miles
Nº of Steam Locos: 10
Nº of Other Locos: 11
Nº of Members: 5,000
Annual Membership Fee: £25.00
Approx Nº of Visitors P.A.: 150,000
Gauge: Standard

SPECIAL INFORMATION

The aim of the GCR is to recreate the experience of
British main line railway operation during the best
years of steam locomotives.

OPERATING INFORMATION

Opening Times: Open daily throughout the year.
Steam Working: Weekends and Bank Holidays
throughout the year. Also weekdays from 15th –
16th April, 29th May to 29th August, 18th – 21st
October and 23rd to 31st December.
Prices: Adult Return £11.00
Child/Senior Citizen Return £7.50
Family Ticket £27.50 (2 adults + 3 children)

GENERAL INFORMATION

Nearest Mainline Station: Loughborough (1 mile)
Nearest Bus Station: Loughborough (½ mile)
Car Parking: Street parking outside the Station
Coach Parking: Car parks at Quorn & Woodhouse,
Rothley and Leicester North
Souvenir Shop(s): Yes
Food & Drinks: Yes – Buffet or Restaurant cars are
usually available for snacks or other meals

Web site: www.gcrailway.co.uk

Detailed Directions by Car:
Great Central Road is on the South East side of Loughborough and is clearly signposted from the A6 Leicester
Road and A60 Nottingham Road.

GREAT WHIPSNADE RAILWAY

Address: Whipsnade Wild Animal Park, Dunstable   LU6 2LF
Telephone N°: (01582) 872171
Year Formed: 1970
Location of Line: Whipsnade Zoo, Near Dunstable
Length of Line: 1¾ miles

N° of Steam Locos: 3
N° of Other Locos: 4
N° of Members: None
Approx N° of Visitors P.A.: 130,000
Gauge: 2 feet 6 inches
Web site: www.whipsnade.co.uk

GENERAL INFORMATION

Nearest Mainline Station: Luton (7 miles)
Nearest Bus Station: Dunstable (3 miles)
Car Parking: Available just outside the park
Coach Parking: Available just outside the park
Souvenir Shop(s): None
Food & Drinks: Available

SPECIAL INFORMATION

The Railway is situated in the Whipsnade Wild Animal Park.

OPERATING INFORMATION

Opening Times: Daily from 10.00am to 6.00pm throughout the year.
Steam Working: Weekends and during School Holidays only.
Prices: Adult Return £2.30
          Child Return £1.80

Detailed Directions by Car:
From All Parts: Exit the M1 at Junction 11 and take the A505 then the B489. Follow signs for Whipsnade Zoo.

GROUDLE GLEN RAILWAY

Address: Groudle Glen, Onchan, Isle of Man	**Nº of Steam Locos:** 2
Telephone Nº: (01624) 670453 (weekends)	**Nº of Other Locos:** 2
Year Formed: 1982 **Re-Opened:** 1986	**Nº of Members:** 600
Location of Line: Groudle Glen	**Annual Membership Fee:** £10.00
Length of Line: ¾ mile	**Approx Nº of Visitors P.A.:** 10,000
Gauge: Narrow	**Correspondence:** 29 Hawarden Avenue, Douglas, Isle of Man IM1 4BP

GENERAL INFORMATION

Nearest Mainline Station: Manx Electric Railway
Nearest Bus Station: Douglas Bus Station
Car Parking: At the entrance to the Glen
Coach Parking: At the entrance to the Glen
Souvenir Shop(s): Yes
Food & Drinks: Coffee and Tea available

SPECIAL INFORMATION

The Railway runs through a picturesque glen to a coastal headland where there are the remains of a Victorian Zoo. The Railway was built in 1896 and closed in 1962.

OPERATING INFORMATION

Opening Times: Easter Sunday & Monday + Sundays from 2nd May to 26th September 11.00am to 4.30pm. Also 3rd, 10th, 17th and 24th August + Wednesday evenings from 7th July to 25th August 7.00pm to 9.00pm. Santa trains run on 12th, 18th and 19th December between 11.00am and 3.30pm + Boxing Day from 12.00pm to 3.30pm
Steam Working: Phone the Railway for details.
Prices: Adult Return £2.00
Child Return £1.00

Detailed Directions by Car:
The Railway is situated on the coast road to the north of Douglas.

GWILI RAILWAY

Address: Bronwydd Arms Station, Bronwydd Arms, Carmarthen   SA33 6HT
Telephone Nº: (01267) 230666
Year Formed: 1975
Location of Line: Near Carmarthen, South Wales
Length of Line: 2½ miles

Nº of Steam Locos: 5
Nº of Other Locos: 6
Nº of Members: 900 shareholders, 450 Society members
Annual Membership Fee: £10.00
Approx Nº of Visitors P.A.: 24,000
Gauge: Standard

GENERAL INFORMATION

Nearest Mainline Station: Carmarthen (3 miles)
Nearest Bus Station: Carmarthen (3 miles)
Car Parking: Free parking at Bronwydd Arms except for a few special occasions
Coach Parking: Free parking at Bronwydd Arms (but by arrangement only)
Souvenir Shop(s): Yes
Food & Drinks: Yes

SPECIAL INFORMATION

Gwili Railway was the first Standard Gauge preserved railway in Wales. There is a riverside picnic area and Miniature railway at Llwyfan Cerrig Station.
Web site: www.gwili-railway.co.uk

OPERATING INFORMATION

Opening Times: Daily from 31st July to 31st August. Open over Easter, on Sundays in May, June, July & September and Wednesdays in June & July. Also open during school half-terms and dates in December. Please phone for further details.
Steam Working: Most advertised trains are steam hauled. Trains run from 11.15am to 4.30pm.
Prices: Adult £5.00
Child £3.00
Family £13.00 (2 adults + up to 2 children)
Senior Citizens £3.00

Detailed Directions by Car:
The Railway is three miles North of Carmarthen – signposted off the A484 Carmarthen to Cardigan Road.

HEATHERSLAW LIGHT RAILWAY

Address: Ford Forge, Heatherslaw, Cornhill-on-Tweed   TD12 4TJ
Telephone N°: (01890) 820244
Year Formed: 1989
Location of Line: Ford & Etal Estates between Wooler & Berwick
Length of Line: 2 miles

N° of Steam Locos: 1
N° of Other Locos: 1
N° of Members: None
Approx N° of Visitors P.A.: 30,000
Gauge: 15 inches
Web site: www.ford-and-etal.co.uk
or   www.secretkingdom.com

GENERAL INFORMATION

Nearest Mainline Station: Berwick-upon-Tweed (10 miles)
Nearest Bus Station: Berwick-upon-Tweed (10 mls)
Car Parking: Available on site
Coach Parking: Available on site
Souvenir Shop(s): Yes
Food & Drinks: Available

SPECIAL INFORMATION

The Railway follows the River Till from Heatherslaw to Etal Village. All coaching stock is built on site.

OPERATING INFORMATION

Opening Times: Daily from the 1st April to 31st October. Trains run hourly from 11.00am to 3.00pm
Steam Working: Daily except when maintenance is is being carried out on the engine.
Prices: Adult Return £5.00
          Child Return £3.00   (Under 5's: £1.00)
          OAP Return £4.00

Detailed Directions by Car:
From the North: Take the A697 from Coldstream and the railway is about 5 miles along; From the South: Take the A697 from Wooler and Millfield.

HOLLYCOMBE STEAM COLLECTION

Address: Hollycombe, Liphook, Hants. GU30 7LP
Telephone Nº: (01428) 724900
Year Formed: 1970
Location of Line: Hollycombe, Liphook
Length of Line: 1¾ miles Narrow gauge, ¼ mile Standard gauge

Nº of Steam Locos: 3
Nº of Other Locos: 1
Nº of Members: 100
Annual Membership Fee: £8.00
Approx Nº of Visitors P.A.: 35,000
Gauge: 2 feet (narrow gauge)
Web site: www.hollycombe.co.uk

GENERAL INFORMATION

Nearest Mainline Station: Liphook (1 mile)
Nearest Bus Station: Liphook
Car Parking: Extensive grass area
Coach Parking: Hardstanding for several
Souvenir Shop(s): Yes
Food & Drinks: Yes – Cafe

SPECIAL INFORMATION

The narrow gauge railway ascends to spectacular views of the Downs and is part of an extensive working steam museum.

OPERATING INFORMATION

Opening Times: Sundays & Bank Holidays from 4th April to 10th October. Open daily from 1st to 30th August.
Steam Working: 1.00pm to 5.00pm
Prices: Adult £8.50
Child £7.00
Family £28.00 (4 people with no more than 2 adults)
Note: Prices are £1.00 less on Summer weekdays

Detailed Directions by Car:
Follow A3 to Liphook and follow the brown tourist signs.

ISLE OF MAN STEAM RAILWAY

Address: Isle of Man Transport, Banks Circus, Douglas, Isle of Man   IM1 5PT
Telephone Nº: (01624) 663366
Year Formed: 1873
Location of Line: Douglas to Port Erin
Length of Line: 15½ miles

Nº of Steam Locos: 6
Nº of Other Locos: 1
Nº of Members: –
Annual Membership Fee: –
Approx Nº of Visitors P.A.: 100,000
Gauge: 3 feet

GENERAL INFORMATION

Nearest Mainline Station: Not applicable
Car Parking: Limited parking at all stations
Coach Parking: Available at Douglas & Port Erin
Souvenir Shop(s): None
Food & Drinks: Yes – Douglas & Port Erin stations

SPECIAL INFORMATION

The Isle of Man Steam Railway is operated by the Isle of Man Government.

OPERATING INFORMATION

Opening Times: Daily from early May to 31st October.
Steam Working: All scheduled services
Prices: Prices vary with 1, 3, 5 & 7 day Explorer tickets also available which include travel on buses, the Snaefell and Manx Electric Railways and Douglas Corporation Horse Trams.

Detailed Directions:
By Sea from Heysham (Lancashire) or Liverpool to reach Isle of Man. By Air from Belfast, Dublin, Glasgow, Edinburgh and other major UK Airports. Douglas Station is ½ mile inland from the Sea terminal and promenade (fully signposted).

ISLE OF WIGHT STEAM RAILWAY

Address: The Railway Station, Haven Street, Ryde, Isle of Wight PO33 4DS	**N° of Other Locos**: 3
Telephone N°: (01983) 882204	**N° of Members**: 1,300
Year Formed: 1971 (re-opened)	**Annual Membership Fee**: £15.00
Location: Smallbrook Junction to Wootton	**Approx N° of Visitors P.A.**: 100,000
Length of Line: 5 miles	**Gauge**: Standard
N° of Steam Locos: 6	**Talking Timetable**: (01983) 882204
	Web site: www.iwsteamrailway.co.uk

GENERAL INFORMATION

Nearest Mainline Station: Smallbrook Junction (direct interchange)
Nearest Bus: From Ryde & Newport direct
Car Parking: Free parking at Havenstreet & Wootton Stations
Coach Parking: Free at Havenstreet Station
Souvenir Shop(s): Yes – at Havenstreet Station
Food & Drinks: Yes – at Havenstreet Station

SPECIAL INFORMATION

The IWSR uses mostly Victorian & Edwardian locomotives and carriages to recreate the atmosphere of an Isle of Wight branch line railway.

OPERATING INFORMATION

Opening Times: Selected days between March and October and daily from 29th May to 19th September
Steam Working: 10.30am to 4.00pm (depending on the Station)
Prices: Adult Return £8.00
Child Return £4.00
Family Return £20.00
(2 adults + 2 children)

Detailed Directions by Car:
To reach the Isle of Wight head for the Ferry ports at Lymington, Southampton or Portsmouth. From all parts of the Isle of Wight, head for Ryde and follow the brown tourist signs.

KEIGHLEY & WORTH VALLEY RAILWAY

Address: The Station, Haworth, Keighley, West Yorkshire   BD22 8NJ
Telephone Nº: (01535) 645214 (enquiries); (01535) 647777 (24 hour timetable)
Year Formed: 1962 (Line re-opened 1968)
Location of Line: From Keighley southwards through Haworth to Oxenhope
Length of Line: 4¾ miles

Nº of Steam Locos: 30
Nº of Other Locos: 10
Members: 4,500 (350 working members)
Annual Membership Fee: Adult £15.00; Adult life membership £300.00
Approx Nº of Visitors P.A.: 150,000
Gauge: Standard
Web Site: www.kwvr.co.uk

GENERAL INFORMATION

Nearest Mainline Station: Keighley (adjacent)
Nearest Bus Station: Keighley (5 minutes walk)
Car Parking: Parking at Keighley, Ingrow, Haworth (charged) and Oxenhope
Coach Parking: At Ingrow & Oxenhope (phone in advance)
Souvenir Shop(s): Yes – at Keighley, Haworth & Oxenhope
Food & Drinks: Yes – at Keighley & Oxenhope when trains run.

OPERATING INFORMATION

Opening Times: Weekends & Bank Holidays throughout the year. Daily from 3rd July to 3rd September. Also open during Easter, Whit, October School holidays and 26th December to 1st January.
Steam Working: Early trains are Diesel; Steam runs from mid-morning on all operating days (except 4 weekends prior to Christmas).
Prices: Adult Return £7.00; £10.00 day rover
  Child Return £3.50; £5.00 day rover
  Family Return £19.00 (2 adults, 3 children)
  Family Day Rover £25.00

Detailed Directions by Car:
Exit the M62 at Junction 26 and take the M606 to its' end. Follow the ring-road signs around Bradford to Shipley. Take the A650 through Bingley to Keighley and follow the brown tourist signs to the railway. Alternatively, take the A6033 from Hebden Bridge to Oxenhope and follow the brown signs to Oxenhope or Haworth Stations.

KENT & EAST SUSSEX RAILWAY

Address: Tenterden Town Station, Tenterden, Kent TN30 6HE	**N° of Steam Locos**: 12
Telephone N°: (01580) 765155	**N° of Other Locos**: 6
Year Formed: 1973	**N° of Members**: 3,000
Location of Line: Tenterden, Kent to Bodiam, East Sussex	**Annual Membership Fee**: £20.00
	Approx N° of Visitors P.A.: 110,000
Length of Line: 10½ miles	**Gauge**: Standard
	Web site: www.kesr.org.uk

GENERAL INFORMATION

Nearest Mainline Station: Headcorn (8 miles)
Nearest Bus Station: Tenterden
Car Parking: Free parking available at Tenderden Town and Northiam Stations
Coach Parking: Tenderden & Northiam
Souvenir Shop(s): Yes
Food & Drinks: Yes

SPECIAL INFORMATION

Built as Britain's first light railway, the K&ESR opened in 1900 and was epitomised by sharp curved and steep gradients and to this day retains a charm and atmosphere all of its own.

OPERATING INFORMATION

Opening Times: From March to October and in December. The return journey time is 1 hour 55 minutes. Please phone the 24 hour talking-timetable for precise operating information: (01580) 762943
Steam Working: Every operational day
Prices: Adult Ticket – £10.00
Child Ticket – £5.00
Family Ticket – £25.00
Note: The prices shown above are for Day Rover tickets which allow unlimited travel on the day of purchase.

Detailed Directions by Car:
From London and Kent Coast: Travel to Ashford (M20) then take the A28 to Tenterden; From Sussex Coast: Take A28 from Hastings to Northiam.

KIRKLEES LIGHT RAILWAY

Address: Park Mill Way, Clayton West, near Huddersfield, W. Yorks.   HD8 9XJ
Telephone Nº: (01484) 865727
Year Formed: 1991
Location of Line: Clayton West to Shelley
Length of Line: 4 miles

Nº of Steam Locos: 4
Nº of Other Locos: 2
Nº of Members: –
Approx Nº of Visitors P.A.: –
Gauge: 15 inches
Web site: www.kirkleeslightrailway.com

GENERAL INFORMATION

Nearest Mainline Station: Denby Dale (4 miles)
Nearest Bus Station: Bus stop outside gates. Take 484 from Wakefield or 235 from Huddersfield/ Barnsley.
Car Parking: Ample free parking at site
Coach Parking: Ample free parking at site
Souvenir Shop(s): Yes
Food & Drinks: Yes

SPECIAL INFORMATION

A new station and visitor centre opened in 1998.

OPERATING INFORMATION

Opening Times: Open every weekend (except 25/26 December) and most school holidays in the Winter. Open daily from 31st May to 3rd September.
Steam Working: All trains are steam-hauled.
Trains run hourly from 11.00am
Prices: Adults £5.50
  Children (3-15 years) £3.50
  Children (under 3 years) Free of charge
  Family Ticket £16.00

Detailed Directions by Car:
The Railway is located on the A636 Wakefield to Denby Dale road. Turn off the M1 at Junction 38 and the railway is 4 miles on the left after going under the railway bridge, just before the village of Scissett.

LAKESIDE & HAVERTHWAITE RAILWAY

Address: Haverthwaite Station, near Ulverston, Cumbria   LA12 8AL
Telephone Nº: (015395) 31594
Year Formed: 1973
Location of Line: Haverthwaite to Lakeside
Length of Line: 3½ miles

Nº of Steam Locos: 8
Nº of Other Locos: 6
Nº of Members: 250
Annual Membership Fee: £10.00 Adult, £5.00 Juniors
Approx Nº of Visitors P.A.: 170,000
Gauge: Standard

GENERAL INFORMATION

Nearest Mainline Station: Ulverston (7 miles)
Nearest Bus Station: Haverthwaite (100 yards)
Car Parking: Plenty of spaces – £1.00 charge
Coach Parking: Free parking at site
Souvenir Shop(s): Yes
Food & Drinks: Yes

SPECIAL INFORMATION

Connections are available at Lakeside for Windermere Lake Cruises to Bowness & Ambleside. Through tickets are available.

OPERATING INFORMATION

Opening Times: Daily from 3rd April to 31st October inclusive. Santa Specials run on 4th, 5th, 11th, 12th, 18th & 19th of December.
Steam Working: Daily from morning to late afternoon.
Prices: Adult Return £4.50; Single £2.70
            Child Return £2.25; Single £1.85
            Family Ticket £12.60

Web site: www.lakesiderailway.co.uk

Detailed Directions by Car:
From All Parts: Exit the M6 at Junction 36 and follow the brown tourist signs.

LAPPA VALLEY STEAM RAILWAY

Address: St. Newlyn East, Newquay, Cornwall TR8 5HZ
Telephone Nº: (01872) 510317
Year Formed: 1974
Location of Line: Benny Halt to East Wheal Rose, near St. Newlyn East
Length of Line: 1 mile

Nº of Steam Locos: 2
Nº of Other Locos: 2
Nº of Members: –
Annual Membership Fee: –
Approx Nº of Visitors P.A.: 50,000
Gauge: 15 inches
Web site: www.lappavalley.co.uk

GENERAL INFORMATION

Nearest Mainline Station: Newquay (5 miles)
Nearest Bus Station: Newquay (5 miles)
Car Parking: Free parking at Benny Halt
Coach Parking: Free parking at Benny Halt
Souvenir Shop(s): Yes
Food & Drinks: Yes

SPECIAL INFORMATION

The railway runs on part of the former Newquay to Chacewater branch line. Site also has a Grade II listed mine building, boating, play areas for children and 2 other miniature train rides.

OPERATING INFORMATION

Opening Times: 6th April to 29th October (daily to 2nd October). Limited opening during October – please phone the Railway for further details.
Steam Working: 10.30am to 4.30pm or later on operating days
Prices: Adult £6.20
Child £4.20
Senior Citizens £5.20
Family £18.50
(2 adults + 2 children)

Detailed Directions by Car:
The railway is signposted from the A30 at the Summercourt-Mitchell bypass, from the A3075 south of Newquay and the A3058 east of Newquay.

LAUNCESTON STEAM RAILWAY

Address: The Old Gasworks, St. Thomas' Road, Launceston, Cornwall   PL15 8DA
Telephone No: (01566) 775665
Year Formed: Opened in 1983
Location of Line: Launceston to Newmills
Length of Line: 2½ miles

No of Steam Locos: 5 (3 working)
No of Other Locos: 2 Diesel, 1 Electric
No of Members: –
Annual Membership Fee: –
Gauge: 1 foot 11 ⅝ inches

GENERAL INFORMATION

Nearest Mainline Station: Liskeard (15 miles)
Nearest Bus Station: Launceston (½ mile) – Devon Bus services stop at the Railway on Sundays only
Car Parking: At Station, Newport Industrial Estate, Launceston
Coach Parking: As above
Souvenir Shop(s): Yes – also with a bookshop
Food & Drinks: Yes – Cafe, snacks & drinks

SPECIAL INFORMATION

During the Summer school holidays, two engines are sometimes in operation. On Sundays, Dartmoor and Tamar Valley 'Rover Tickets' are available.

OPERATING INFORMATION

Opening Times: Good Friday for 8 days then Sundays and Tuesdays until Whit. Open from Sundays to Wednesdays in June and Sundays to Fridays from July to September. Also during half-term in October.
Steam Working: 11.00am to 4.30pm on operational days
Prices: Adult £6.50
              Child £4.25
              Family £20.00 (2 adults + 4 children)
              Senior Citizen £5.00
Group rates are available upon application. These prices include as many trips as you like on the day of purchase.

Detailed Directions by Car:
Drive to Launceston and look for the brown Steam Engine Tourist signs. Use the L.S.R. car park at the Newport Industrial Estate.

THE LAVENDER LINE

Address: Isfield Station, Isfield, near Uckfield, East Sussex TN22 5XB	**Nº of Steam Locos**: 2
Telephone Nº: (01825) 750515	**Nº of Other Locos**: 16
Year Formed: 1992	**Nº of Members**: Approximately 400
Location of Line: East Sussex between Lewes and Uckfield	**Annual Membership Fee**: £10.00
	Approx Nº of Visitors P.A.: 12,500
Length of Line: ¾ mile	**Gauge**: Standard
	Web site: www.lavender-line.co.uk

GENERAL INFORMATION

Nearest Mainline Station: Uckfield (3 miles)
Nearest Bus Station: Uckfield (3 miles)
Car Parking: Free parking at site
Coach Parking: Can cater for coach parties – please contact the Railway.
Souvenir Shop: Yes
Food & Drinks: Yes – Cinders Buffet

SPECIAL INFORMATION

Isfield Station has been restored as a Southern Railway country station complete with the original L.B.S.C.R. signalbox.

Information Line: (09068) 800645 (60p/minute)

OPERATING INFORMATION

Opening Times: Sundays throughout the year. Saturdays and Sundays in June, July and August plus Wednesdays and Thursdays in August. Also open on Bank Holidays and in December for Santa Specials.
Steam Working: Please phone for details.
Prices: Adult £5.00
Child £3.00
Senior Citizen £4.00
Family (2 adults + 3 children) £14.00
All tickets offer unlimited rides on the day of issue and prices may vary on special event days.

Detailed Directions by Car::
From All Parts: Isfield is just off the A26 midway between Lewes and Uckfield.

LEIGHTON BUZZARD RAILWAY

Address: Pages Park Station, Billington Road, Leighton Buzzard, Beds. LU7 4TN
Telephone Nº: (01525) 373888
Year Formed: 1967
Location of Line: Leighton Buzzard
Length of Line: 3 miles

Nº of Steam Locos: 12
Nº of Other Locos: 41
Nº of Members: 400
Annual Membership Fee: £16.00
Approx Nº of Visitors P.A.: 21,000
Gauge: 2 feet

GENERAL INFORMATION

Nearest Mainline Station: Leighton Buzzard (2 miles)
Nearest Bus Station: Leighton Buzzard (¾ mile)
Car Parking: Free parking adjacent
Coach Parking: Free parking adjacent
Souvenir Shop(s): Yes
Food & Drinks: Yes

Web site: www.buzzrail.co.uk

OPERATING INFORMATION

Opening Times: Sundays from 14th March to 31st October plus Bank Holiday weekends. Also open on some Saturdays and weekdays. Trains run from mid-morning to late afternoon and Santa Specials run on some dates in December.
Steam Working: Most operating days.
Prices: Adult £5.50
Child £2.50
Senior Citizens £4.50

Detailed Directions by Car:
The railway is 15 minutes drive from Junctions 11-13 of the M1. Follow the brown tourist signs in Leighton Buzzard or from the A505. Pages Park Station is ¾ mile from the Town Centre on the A4146 Hemel Hempstead road.

LINCOLNSHIRE WOLDS RAILWAY

Address: The Railway Station, Ludborough, Lincolnshire   DN36 5SQ
Telephone Nº: (01507) 363881
Year Formed: 1979
Location of Line: Ludborough – off the A16(T) between Grimsby and Louth
Length of Line: ¾ mile

Nº of Steam Locos: 3   **Other Locos**: 7
Nº of Members of the Supporting Society (GLRPS): 400+
Annual Membership Fee: £14.00 Family, £7.00 Adult, £4.50 Senior Citizen or Child
Approx Nº of Visitors P.A.: 5,000
Gauge: Standard

GENERAL INFORMATION

Nearest Mainline Station: Grimsby (8 miles)
Nearest Bus Stop: Ludborough (½ mile)
Car Parking: 100 spaces for cars at the Station
Coach Parking: Space for 1 coach only
Souvenir Shop(s): Yes
Food & Drinks: Yes

SPECIAL INFORMATION

The buildings and facilities at Ludborough have been completed and short steam trips commenced in 1998. Plans to extend the line to North Thoresby (1 mile) are being pursued.

OPERATING INFORMATION

Opening Times: Certain Sundays from January to December. Also Santa Specials in December. Advance bookings are essential.
Steam Working: Contact the Railway for details.
Prices: Adults £3.00
      Senior Citizens/Children £1.50
      Family £7.00 (2 adults + 4 children)
Different fares may apply at Special Events. Day tickets are available on request.

Web site: www.lincolnshirewoldsrailway.co.uk

Detailed Directions by Car:
The Railway is situated near Ludborough, ½ mile off the A16(T) Louth to Grimsby road. Follow signs to Fulstow to reach the station (approximately ½ mile). Do not turn into Ludborough but stay on the bypass.

LLANBERIS LAKE RAILWAY

Address: Gilfach Ddu, Llanberis, Gwynedd LL55 4TY	**Nº of Steam Locos**: 3
Telephone Nº: (01286) 870549	**Nº of Other Locos**: 4
Year Formed: 1970	**Nº of Members**: –
Location of Line: Just off the A4086 Caernarfon to Capel Curig road at Llanberis	**Annual Membership Fee**: –
	Approx Nº of Visitors P.A.: 70,000
Length of Line: 2½ miles	**Gauge**: 1 foot 11½ inches
	Web site: www.lake-railway.co.uk

GENERAL INFORMATION

Nearest Mainline Station: Bangor (8 miles)
Nearest Bus Station: Caernarfon (6 miles)
Car Parking: £1.50 Council car park on site
Coach Parking: Ample free parking on site
Souvenir Shop(s): Yes
Food & Drinks: Yes

SPECIAL INFORMATION

Llanberis Lake Railway runs along part of the trackbed of the Padarn Railway which transported slates for export and closed in 1961. An extension to Llanberis village opened in June 2003.

OPERATING INFORMATION

Opening Times: Open most days from mid-March to 31st October. Please send for a free timetable.
Steam Working: 11.30am to 4.30pm on most days.
Prices: Adult £6.00
　　　　　Child £4.00
Various Family ticket options are available.
N.B. The Welsh Slate Museum is adjacent to the Railway.

Detailed Directions by Car:
The railway is situated just off the A4086 Caernarfon to Capel Curig road. Follow signs for Padarn Country Park.

LLANGOLLEN RAILWAY

Address: The Station, Abbey Road, Llangollen, Denbighshire LL20 8SN	**N° of Steam Locos:** 14
Telephone N°: (01978) 860979	**N° of Other Locos:** 13
Year Formed: 1975	**N° of Members:** 1,300
Location of Line: Valley of the River Dee from Llangollen to Carrog	**Annual Membership Fee:** Adult £13.00; Family £20.00; Junior (under-16) £8.00
Length of Line: 7½ miles	**Approx N° of Visitors P.A.:** 90,000
	Gauge: Standard

GENERAL INFORMATION

Nearest Mainline Station: Ruabon (6 miles)
Nearest Bus Station: Wrexham (12 miles)
Car Parking: Public car park at Lower Dee Mill off A539 Ruabon road.
Coach Parking: Market Street car park in town centre
Souvenir Shop(s): Yes – at Llangollen Station
Food & Drinks: Yes – at Llangollen, Berwyn, Glyndyfrdwy and Carrog Stations.

SPECIAL INFORMATION

The route originally formed part of the line from Ruabon to Barmouth Junction, closed in 1964. The railway has been rebuilt by volunteers since 1975, reopening to Carrog in 1996.
The ultimate aim is to reopen to Corwen (10 miles).

OPERATING INFORMATION

Opening Times: Services run daily from 9th April to 31st October (except on Mondays in October). Also on weekends from late November to 2nd January.
Steam Working: Phone the Talking timetable number for further details: (01978) 860951
Prices: Adult Return £8.00 (Llangollen to Carrog)
Child Return £4.00
Family £18.00 (2 adults + 2 children)
Senior Citizens £6.00

Web Site: www.llangollen-railway.co.uk

Detailed Directions by Car:
From South & West: Go via the A5 to Llangollen. At the traffic lights turn into Castle Street to the River bridge; From North & East: Take the A483 to A539 junction and then via Trefor to Llangollen River bridge. The Station is adjacent to the River Dee.

MANGAPPS RAILWAY MUSEUM

Address: Southminster Road, Burnham-on-Crouch, Essex CM0 8QQ	**N° of Steam Locos**: 6
Telephone N°: (01621) 784898	**N° of Other Locos**: 7
Year Formed: 1989	**N° of Members**: –
Location of Line: Mangapps Farm	**Annual Membership Fee**: –
Length of Line: ¾ mile	**Approx N° of Visitors P.A.**: 20,000
	Gauge: Standard

GENERAL INFORMATION

Nearest Mainline Station: Burnham-on-Crouch (1 mile)
Nearest Bus Station: –
Car Parking: Ample free parking at site
Coach Parking: Ample free parking at site
Souvenir Shop(s): Yes
Food & Drinks: Yes – drinks and snacks only

SPECIAL INFORMATION

The Railway endeavours to recreate the atmosphere of an East Anglian light railway. It also includes an extensive museum with an emphasis on East Anglian items and signalling.

Web Site: www.mangapps.co.uk

OPERATING INFORMATION

Opening Times: Closed during January, then open every weekend and bank holiday (except over Christmas). Open every day during the Easter Fortnight and August. Special events in 2004: 'Day Out With Thomas' May 1st/2nd/3rd/8th/9th, July 3rd/4th/10th/11th and November 6th/7th/13th/14th. Santa Specials run during weekends in December.
Steam Working: Every Sunday during August and December plus bank holidays. Diesel at other times.
Prices: Adult – Steam £5.50; Diesel £4.50
Child – Steam £3.00; Diesel £2.50
N.B. Prices for special events may differ.

Detailed Directions by Car:
From South & West: From M25 take either the A12 or A127 and then the A130 to Rettendon Turnpike and then follow signs to Burnham; From North: From A12 take A414 to Oak Corner then follow signs to Burnham.

THE MIDDLETON RAILWAY

Address: The Station, Moor Road, Hunslet, Leeds LS10 2JQ
Telephone N⁰: (0113) 271-0320
Year Formed: 1960
Location of Line: Moor Road to Middleton Park
Length of Line: 1½ miles

N⁰ of Steam Locos: 15
N⁰ of Other Locos: 12
Annual Membership Fee: Adults £9.50
Approx N⁰ of Visitors P.A.: 20,000
Gauge: Standard
Web Site: www.middletonrailway.org.uk

GENERAL INFORMATION

Nearest Mainline Station: Leeds City (1 mile)
Nearest Bus Station: Leeds (1½ miles)
Car Parking: Free parking at site
Coach Parking: Free parking at site
Souvenir Shop(s): Yes
Food & Drinks: Yes

SPECIAL INFORMATION

The Middleton Railway is the world's oldest working railway, founded in 1758. Passenger services run from the station into Middleton Park. A large collection of preserved industrial steam and diesel engines are displayed, many of them more than 100 years old.

OPERATING INFORMATION

Opening Times: Open 10.30am to 5.00pm Weekends & Bank Holidays from 27th March to 19th December. Also opens for "Thomas", Santa Specials and other events – phone the railway for further details.
Steam Working: 11.00am to 4.20pm on Sundays and Bank Holidays.
Prices: Adult £2.50
Child £1.50
Family £7.00
(2 adults + 2 children)
Tickets provide for unlimited travel on the day of issue.
Please send SAE for the timetable and details of special events.

Detailed Directions by Car:
From the M1 Northbound: Take the M621 from Leeds City Centre and exit at Junction 5, turn right at the top of the slip road and take 3rd exit at the roundabout. The entrance to the Railway is 50 yards on the right. The railway is also signposted from the A61 and A653.

MID-HANTS RAILWAY (WATERCRESS LINE)

Address: The Railway Station, Alresford, Hampshire SO24 9JG
Telephone Nº: (01962) 733810 General enquiries; (01962) 734866 Timetable
Year Formed: 1977
Location of Line: Alresford to Alton
Length of Line: 10 miles

Nº of Steam Locos: 16
Nº of Other Locos: 8
Nº of Members: 4,500
Annual Membership Fee: Adult £17.50
Approx Nº of Visitors P.A.: 130,000
Gauge: Standard
Web Site: www.watercressline.co.uk

GENERAL INFO

Nearest Mainline Station: Alton (adjacent) or Winchester (7 miles)
Nearest Bus Station: Winchester
Car Parking: Pay and display at Alton and Alresford Stations (Alresford free on Sundays & Bank Holidays)
Coach Parking: By arrangement at Alresford Station
Souvenir Shop(s): At Alresford, Ropley & Alton
Food & Drinks: Yes – Buffet on most trains. 'West Country' buffet at Alresford

SPECIAL INFO

The railway runs through four fully restored stations and has a Loco yard and picnic area at Ropley.

OPERATING INFO

Opening Times: Weekends and Bank Holidays from January to November. Weekdays from May to September and during School Holidays. Weekends and other dates in December.
Steam Working: All operating days.
Prices: Adult £10.00
　　　　　Child (age 3 to 16) £5.00
　　　　　Senior Citizens £9.00
　　　　　Family £25.00
　　　　　(2 adults + 2 children)
A discount is available for pre-booked parties of 15 or more people. Write or call for a booking form.

Detailed Directions by Car:
From the East: Take the M25 then A3 and A31 to Alton; From the West: Exit the M3 at Junction 9 and take the A31 to Alresford Station.

MIDLAND RAILWAY – BUTTERLEY

Address: Butterley Station, Ripley, Derbyshire DE5 3QZ	**No of Steam Locos**: 25
Telephone No: (01773) 747674	**No of Other Locos**: 53
Year Formed: 1969	**No of Members**: 2,000
Location of Line: Butterley, near Ripley	**Annual Membership Fee**: £14.00
Length of Line: Standard gauge 3½ miles, Narrow gauge 0.8 mile	**Approx No of Visitors P.A.**: 130,000
	Gauge: Standard, various Narrow gauges and miniature

GENERAL INFORMATION

Nearest Mainline Station: Alfreton (6 miles)
Nearest Bus Station: Bus stop outside Butterley Station.
Car Parking: Free parking at site – ample space
Coach Parking: Free parking at site
Souvenir Shop(s): Yes – at Butterley and Swanwick
Food & Drinks: Yes – both sites + bar on train

SPECIAL INFORMATION

The Centre is a unique project with a huge Museum development together with narrow gauge, miniature & model railways as well as a country park and farm park. Includes an Award-winning Victorian Railwayman's church and Princess Royal Class Locomotive Trust Depot.

OPERATING INFORMATION

Opening Times: The centre is open daily – trains do not run every day it is open however.
Steam Working: Weekends and bank holidays throughout the year. Thursdays June to September and most days in the school holidays. Phone for further details. 'Day Out With Thomas' 2004 events: 6th, 7th, 13th & 16th March; 29th May to 6th June; 4th to 8th August and 16th & 17th October.
Prices: Adult £8.95   Senior Citizens £7.95
   Children £4.50

Detailed Directions by Car:
From All Parts: From the M1 exit at Junction 28 and take the A38 towards Derby. The Centre is signposted at the junction with the B6179.

MOORS VALLEY RAILWAY

Address: Moors Valley Country Park, Horton Road, Ashley Heath, Nr. Ringwood, Hants. BH24 2ET **Telephone Nº:** (01425) 471415 **Year Formed:** 1985 **Location of Line:** Moors Valley Country Park	**Length of Line:** 1 mile **Nº of Steam Locos:** 14 **Nº of Other Locos:** 1 **Nº of Members:** – **Approx Nº of Visitors P.A.:** – **Gauge:** 7¼ inches **Web site:** www.moorsvalleyrailway.co.uk

GENERAL INFORMATION

Nearest Mainline Station: Bournemouth (12 miles)
Nearest Bus Station: Ringwood (3 miles)
Car Parking: Parking charge varies throughout the year. Maximum charge £5.00 per day.
Coach Parking: Charges are applied for parking
Souvenir Shop(s): Yes + Model Railway Shop
Food & Drinks: Yes

SPECIAL INFORMATION

The Moors Valley Railway is a complete small Railway with signalling and 2 signal boxes and also 4 tunnels and 2 level crossings.

OPERATING INFORMATION

Opening Times: Weekends throughout the year. Daily from one week before to one week after Easter, Spring Bank Holiday to mid-September, during School half-term holidays and also from Boxing Day to end of School holidays. Also Santa Specials in December and occasional other openings. Phone the Railways for details.
Steam Working: 10.45am to 5.00pm when open.
Prices: Adult Return £2.40; Adult Single £1.35
          Child Return £1.70; Child Single 95p
Special rates are available for parties of 10 or more.

Detailed Directions by Car:
From All Parts: Moors Valley Country Park is situated on Horton Road which is off the A31 Ferndown to Ringwood road near the junction with the A338 to Bournemouth.

MULL & WEST HIGHLAND RAILWAY

Address: Old Pier Station, Craignure,
Isle of Mull, Argyll   PA65 6AY
Telephone Nº: (01680) 812494
Web site: www.mullrail.co.uk
Year Formed: 1983
Location of Line: Isle of Mull
Length of Line: 1¼ miles

Gauge: 10¼ inches
Nº of Steam Locos: 2
Nº of Other Locos: 3
Nº of Members: 30 (also Friends of the
Railway)
Annual Membership Fee: £5.00
Approx Nº of Visitors P.A.: 30,000

GENERAL INFORMATION

Nearest Mainline Station: Oban (11 miles by Cal-Mac Ferry)
Nearest Bus Station: Oban (as above)
Car Parking: Free parking on site at Craignure
Coach Parking: Free parking at site
Souvenir Shop(s): Yes
Food & Drinks: No – but drinks & sweets available

SPECIAL INFORMATION

This narrow gauge railway was the first passenger railway to be built on a Scottish island. It was built specially to link Torosay Castle & Gardens to the main Port of entry at Craignure.

OPERATING INFORMATION

Opening Times: Daily from 1st April to 28th October. Opens 11.00am to 5.00pm.
Steam Working: Steam and diesel trains are run depending on operational requirements.
Prices: Adult Single £3.00; Adult Return £4.00
Child Single £2.00; Child Return £3.00
Family Tickets (2 adults + 2 children)
Single £7.50; Return £10.75

Detailed Directions by Car:
Once off the ferry, turn left at the end of the pier, go straight on for almost ½ mile then turn left at the thistle sign opposite the Police station and carry straight on until you reach the station car park.

NENE VALLEY RAILWAY

Address: Wansford Station, Stibbington, Peterborough PE8 6LR	**N° of Steam Locos**: 17
Telephone N°: (01780) 784444 enquiries; (01780) 784404 talking timetable	**N° of Other Locos**: 11
	N° of Members: 1,300
Year Formed: 1977	**Annual Membership Fee**: Adult £11.50; Child £6.50; Joint £18.50; OAP £6.50
Location: Off A1 to west of Peterborough	**Approx N° of Visitors P.A.**: 65,000
Length of Line: 7½ miles	**Gauge**: Standard

GENERAL INFORMATION

Nearest Mainline Station: Peterborough (¾ mile)
Nearest Bus Station: Peterborough (Queensgate – ¾ mile)
Car Parking: Free parking at Wansford & Orton Mere
Coach Parking: Free coach parking at Wansford
Souvenir Shop(s): Yes
Food & Drinks: Yes

SPECIAL INFORMATION

The railway is truly international in flavour with British and Continental locomotives and rolling stock.

Web site: www.nvr.org.uk

OPERATING INFORMATION

Opening Times: Sundays from 8th February to 31st October. Saturdays from Easter to end of October. Mid-week on various dates from May to the end of August and also at various other times. Contact the Railway for complete details. Open 9.00am to 4.30pm.
Steam Working: Most services are steam hauled apart from on diesel days and times of high fire risk.
Prices: Adult £10.00 (Special events £12.00)
Child £5.00 (age 3-15) (Special events £6.00)
Family £25.00 (2 adult + 3 child) (Special £25.00)
Senior Citizens/Disabled £7.50 (Special £9.00)

Detailed Directions by Car:
The railway is situated off the southbound carriageway of the A1 between the A47 and A605 junctions – west of Peterborough and south of Stamford.

Northampton & Lamport Railway

Address: Pitsford & Bramford Station, Pitsford Road, Chapel Brampton, Northampton NN6 8BA **Telephone Nº:** (01604) 820327 (infoline) **Year Formed:** 1983 (became operational in November 1995) **Web site:** www.nlr.org.uk	**Length of Line:** 1¼ miles at present **Nº of Steam Locos:** 6 **Nº of Other Locos:** 9 **Nº of Members:** 650 **Annual Membership Fee:** £10.00 **Approx Nº of Visitors P.A.:** 24,000 **Gauge:** Standard

GENERAL INFORMATION

Nearest Mainline Station: Northampton (5 miles)
Nearest Bus Station: Northampton (5 miles)
Car Parking: Free parking at site
Coach Parking: Free parking at site
Souvenir Shop(s): Yes
Food & Drinks: Yes

SPECIAL INFORMATION

A developing railway – this became operational again on 18th November 1995.

OPERATING INFORMATION

Opening Times: Sundays and Bank holidays from March to October. Santa Specials in December. Open 10.30am to 5.00pm.
Steam Working: Generally between April and September and also in December.
Prices: Adult £3.50
Child £2.50
Family £10.00 (2 adults + 2 children)
Senior Citizen £2.50
Fares may vary on Special Event days.

Detailed Directions by Car:
The station is situated along the Pitsford road at Chapel Brampton, approximately 5 miles north of Northampton. Heading north out of town, it is signposted to the right on the A5199 (A50) Welford Road at Chapel Brampton crossroads or on the left on the A508 Market Harborough road at the Pitsford turn.

NORTH NORFOLK RAILWAY

Address: Sheringham Station, Sheringham, Norfolk NR26 8RA	**Nº of Steam Locos**: 4
Telephone Nº: (01263) 820800	**Nº of Other Locos**: 5
Year Formed: 1975	**Nº of Members**: 1,000
Location of Line: Sheringham to Holt via Weybourne	**Annual Membership Fee**: £12.00
	Approx Nº of Visitors P.A.: 100,000
Length of Line: 5¼ miles	**Gauge**: Standard
	Web site: www.nnr.co.uk

GENERAL INFORMATION

Nearest Mainline Station: Sheringham (200 yards)
Nearest Bus Station: Outside the Station
Car Parking: Adjacent to all three stations
Coach Parking: Adjacent to all three stations
Souvenir Shop(s): Yes – at all three stations
Food & Drinks: Yes – main catering facilities at Sheringham Station

SPECIAL INFORMATION

Sheringham Station has a museum room and signalbox. The railway is the only full-sized preserved Steam railway in Norfolk.

OPERATING INFORMATION

Opening Times: Most days from 29th March to 31st October plus weekends in November and December.
Steam Working: 11.00am to 5.00pm
Prices: Adult £8.00
 Child £4.50 (Under 4's free of charge)
 Family £23.00 (includes free brochure)
 Senior Citizens £7.00
All the above prices are all-day tickets.
Special events: Steam Gala – 3rd to 5th September; 1940's Weekend – 19th and 20th September; Mince Pie Specials – 26th December – 4th January.

Detailed Directions by Car:
The railway is situated on the A149 Cromer to Sheringham road. All 3 stations are signposted from this road.

NORTH SCARLE MINIATURE RAILWAY

Address: North Scarle Playing Field, Swinderby Road, North Scarle, Lincolnshire	**Nº of Steam Locos:** 7
	Nº of Other Locos: 5
	Nº of Members: 35
Telephone Nº: (01522) 888228	**Annual Membership Fee:** £25.00
Year Formed: 1933	**Approx Nº of Visitors P.A.:** 3,000
Location of Line: North Scarle, between Newark and Lincoln	**Gauges:** 7¼ inches and 5 inches
	Web site: www.lincolnmes.co.uk
Length of Line: A third of a mile	

GENERAL INFORMATION

Nearest Mainline Station: Newark Northgate (5 miles)
Nearest Bus Station: Newark (5 miles)
Car Parking: 300 spaces available on site
Coach Parking: None available
Souvenir Shop(s): None
Food & Drinks: Available on special days only

SPECIAL INFORMATION

The Railway is owned and operated by the Lincoln and District Model Engineering Society which was founded in 1933.

OPERATING INFORMATION

Opening Times: Car Boot Sale Sundays only!
Dates for 2004: 28th March; 11th & 25th April; 9th & 23rd May; 6th & 20th June; 4th & 18th July; 1st, 15th & 29th August; 12th, 18th, 19th & 26th September; 10th October.
Steam Working: Every running day.
Prices: Adult Return 40p
      Child Return 40p

Detailed Directions by Car:
North Scarle is situated off the A46 between Lincoln and Newark (about 5 miles from Newark). Alternatively, take the A1133 from Gainsborough and follow the North Scarle signs when around 6 miles from Newark.

NORTH YORKSHIRE MOORS RAILWAY

Address: Pickering Station, Pickering, North Yorkshire YO18 7AJ	**Length of Line**: 18 miles
Telephone Nº: (01751) 472508 (enquiries)	**Nº of Steam Locos**: 20
Web site: www.northyorkshiremoorsrailway.com	**Nº of Other Locos**: 12
Year Formed: 1967	**Nº of Members**: 8,000
Location of Line: Pickering to Grosmont via stations at Levisham and Goathland	**Annual Membership Fee**: Adult £16.00; Over 60's £12.00
	Approx Nº of Visitors P.A.: 280,000
	Gauge: Standard

GENERAL INFORMATION

Nearest Mainline Station: Grosmont (opposite NYMR station)
Nearest Bus Station: Pickering (½ mile)
Car Parking: Available at each station
Coach Parking: Available at Pickering & Grosmont
Souvenir Shop(s): Yes – at Pickering, Goathland and Grosmont
Food & Drinks: Pickering, Grosmont & Goathland

SPECIAL INFORMATION

The NYMR runs through the spectacular North Yorks Moors and is the most popular in the country. As seen in 'Heartbeat' and also used in the filming of the Harry Potter films.

OPERATING INFORMATION

Opening Times: Open daily from 27th March to 31st October.
Steam Working: Usually daily – please phone the Railway for timetable information
Prices: Adult £12.00 (all-day travel)
   Child £6.00 (all-day travel)
Family Tickets start at £25.00 for 2 adults & 1 child –
   £26.00 for 2 adults and 2 children
   £27.00 for 2 adults and 3 children
   £28.00 for 2 adults and 4 children

Detailed Directions by Car:
From the South: Follow signs to York, follow the A64 to the Malton bypass then take the A169 to Pickering; From the North: Take A171 towards Whitby then follow the minor road through Egton to Grosmont.

NOTTINGHAM TRANSPORT HERITAGE CENTRE

Address: Nottingham Transport Heritage Centre, Mere Way, Ruddington, Nottingham NG11 6NX	Loughborough Junction
	Length of Line: 9 miles
	No of Steam Locos: 6
Telephone No: (0115) 940-5705	**No of Other Locos:** 7
Fax No: (0115) 940-5905	**No of Members:** 850
Year Formed: 1990 (Opened in 1994)	**Annual Membership Fee:** £12.00
Location of Line: Ruddington to	**Approx No of Visitors P.A.:** 15,000

GENERAL INFORMATION

Nearest Mainline Station: Nottingham (5 miles)
Nearest Bus Station: Bus service from Nottingham to the Centre
Car Parking: Free parking at site
Coach Parking: Free parking at site
Souvenir Shop(s): Yes
Food & Drinks: Yes

SPECIAL INFORMATION

The Heritage Centre covers an area of over eleven acres and is set within the Rushcliffe Country Park in Ruddington. Trains now run to Rushcliffe Halt.

OPERATING INFORMATION

Opening Times: Sundays and Bank Holidays from 11th April to 3rd October. Open 10.45am to 5.30pm. Also open for Santa Specials on December weekends.
Steam Working: Steam service runs from 11.30am
Prices: Adult £5.00
　　　　　Child £3.00
　　　　　Senior Citizens £4.50
　　　　　Family £15.00 (2 adults + 3 children)

Web Site: www.nthc.co.uk

Detailed Directions by Car:
From All Parts: The centre is situated off the A60 Nottingham to Loughborough Road and is signposted just south of the traffic lights at Ruddington.

PAIGNTON & DARTMOUTH STEAM RAILWAY

Address: Queen's Park Station, Torbay Road, Paignton   TQ4 6AF
Telephone Nº: (01803) 555872
Year Formed: 1973
Location of Line: Paignton to Kingswear
Length of Line: 7 miles

Nº of Steam Locos: 6
Nº of Other Locos: 3
Nº of Members: –
Annual Membership Fee: –
Approx Nº of Visitors P.A.: 350,000
Gauge: Standard

GENERAL INFORMATION

Nearest Mainline Station: Paignton (adjacent)
Nearest Bus Station: Paignton (2 minutes walk)
Car Parking: Multi-storey or Mainline Station
Coach Parking: Multi-storey (3 minutes walk)
Souvenir Shop(s): Yes – at Paignton & Kingswear
Food & Drinks: Yes – at Paignton & Kinswear

SPECIAL INFORMATION

A passenger ferry is available from Kingswear Station across to Dartmouth. Combined excursions are also available including train and river trips.

Web site: www.paignton-steamrailway.co.uk

OPERATING INFORMATION

Opening Times: Open daily from June to September (inclusive). Also open days in April, May, October and December (phone for details).
Steam Working: Trains run throughout the day from 10.30am to 5.00pm
Prices: Adult Return £7.00
          Child Return £5.00
Family Return £22.00 (2 adults + 2 children)

Detailed Directions by Car:
From All Parts: Take the M5 to Exeter and then the A380 to Paignton.

PALLOT STEAM MUSEUM

Address: Rue de Brechet, Trinity, Jersey, JE3 5BE
Telephone Nº: (01534) 865307
Year Formed: 1990
Location of Line: Trinity, Jersey
Length of Line: A third of a mile

Nº of Steam Locos: 4
Nº of Other Locos: 2
Nº of Members: None
Approx Nº of Visitors P.A.: 12,000
Gauge: Standard
Web site: None

GENERAL INFORMATION

Nearest Mainline Station: None
Nearest Bus Station: St. Helier
Car Parking: Available on site
Coach Parking: Available on site
Souvenir Shop(s): Yes
Food & Drinks: Snacks only

SPECIAL INFORMATION

The museum was founded by Lyndon (Don) Pallot who spent his early career as a trainee engineer with the old Jersey Railway.

OPERATING INFORMATION

Opening Times: Daily from 1st April to 31st October. Open from 10.00am to 5.00pm. Closed on Sundays.
Steam Working: Every Thursday and also on high-season Tuesdays.
Prices: Adult Museum Admission £3.50
Child Museum Admission £1.50
Senior Citizen Museum Admission £3.00
Adult Train Ride £1.50
Child Train Ride £1.00

Detailed Directions by Car:
The museum lies between the A8 and the A9 main roads (Bus Route 5 is easiest) and is signposted off both of these roads.

PEAK RAIL PLC

Address: Matlock Station, Matlock, Derbyshire   DE4 3NA
Telephone Nº: (01629) 580381
Fax Nº: (01629) 760645
Year Formed: 1975
Location of Line: Matlock Riverside to Rowsley South

Length of Line: 4½ miles
Nº of Steam Locos: 6 **Other Locos:** 20+
Nº of Members: 1,500
Annual Adult Membership Fee: £12.00
Approx Nº of Visitors P.A.: 30,000
Gauge: Standard
Web site: www.peakrail.co.uk

GENERAL INFORMATION

Nearest Mainline Station: Matlock (500 yards)
Nearest Bus Station: Matlock
Car Parking: Paid car parking at Matlock Station, 200 spaces at Rowsley South Station, 20 spaces at Darley Dale Station
Coach Parking: Free parking at Rowsley South
Souvenir Shop(s): Yes
Food & Drinks: Yes

SPECIAL INFORMATION

The Palatine Restaurant Car is available whilst travelling on the train and caters for Sunday Lunches, Teas and Party Bookings. Coach parties are welcomed when the railway is operating.

OPERATING INFORMATION

Opening Times: Sundays in January-March and November. Weekends during the rest of the year. Also Wednesdays June and July, Tuesdays in July, Tuesdays, Wednesdays and Thursdays in August.
Steam Working: All services throughout the year.
Prices: Adult Return £6.00
  Children – Under-3's free of charge
  Children – Ages 3-5 £1.00
  Children – Ages 6-15 £3.00
  Senior Citizen Return £4.60
  Family Ticket (2 adults + 3 children) £17.00

Detailed Directions by Car:
Exit the M1 at Junctions 28, 29 or 30 and follow signs towards Matlock. From North and South take A6 direct to Matlock. From Stoke-on-Trent, take the A52 to Ashbourne, then the A5035 to Matlock. Upon reaching Matlock follow the brown tourist signs.

PLYM VALLEY RAILWAY

Address: Marsh Mills Station, Coypool Road, Plympton, Plymouth PL7 4NW	**Nº of Steam Locos:** 3
Telephone Nº: (01752) 330881	**Nº of Other Locos:** 3
Year Formed: 1980	**Nº of Members:** 200
Location of Line: Marsh Mills to World's End, Plympton	**Annual Membership Fee:** £10.00
	Approx Nº of Visitors P.A.: 5,000
	Gauge: Standard
Length of Line: ½ mile	**Web site:** www.plymrail.co.uk

GENERAL INFORMATION

Nearest Mainline Station: Plymouth (4 miles)
Nearest Bus Station: Plymouth (3 miles)
Car Parking: Available on site
Coach Parking: Available on site
Souvenir Shop(s): Yes
Food & Drinks: Light snacks available

SPECIAL INFORMATION

It is planned to extend the line to Plymbridge, a distance of 1¼ miles.

OPERATING INFORMATION

Opening Times: Most Sundays from 10.00am to 5.00pm. Not every open day has trains operating, however.
Steam Working: Second Sunday in every month from April to November. Also the fourth Sunday of the month from June to September. Trains run from 1.00pm to 4.00pm.
Prices: Adult Return £1.50
　　　　　 Child Return 75p
Note: There is no charge to visit the station.

Detailed Directions by Car:
Leave the A38 at the Marsh Mills turn-off and take the B3416 towards Plympton. Turn left into Coypool Road just after the McDonalds restaurant. From Plymouth City Centre, take the A374 to Marsh Mills, then as above.

Pontypool & Blaenavon Railway

Address: c/o Council Offices, 101 High
Street, Blaenavon, Torfaen NP4 9PT
Telephone Nº: (01495) 792263 or 760242
Year Formed: 1980 (Opened 1984)
Location of Line: Just off the B4248
between Blaenavon and Brynmawr
Length of Line: ¾ mile

Nº of Steam Locos: 9
Nº of Other Locos: 5
Nº of Members: 190
Annual Membership Fee: £10.00
Approx Nº of Visitors P.A.: 4,000
Gauge: Standard
Web site: www.pontypool-and-blaenavon.co.uk

GENERAL INFORMATION

Nearest Mainline Station: Abergavenny (5 miles)
Nearest Bus Station: Blaenavon Town (1½ miles) –
regular bus service within ¼ mile (except Sundays)
Car Parking: Free parking for 50 cars on site
Coach Parking: Available on site
Souvenir Shop(s): Yes – on the train (usually) and
also a shop at 13 Broad Street, Blaenavon
Food & Drinks: Light refreshments on the train

SPECIAL INFORMATION

The railway operates over very steep gradients, is
run entirely by volunteers and is the highest
standard gauge preserved railway in Wales.

OPERATING INFORMATION

Opening Times: Every Sunday and Bank Holiday
Monday from Easter to the end of September. Santa
Specials and other Special events also run. Please
phone the Railway for details. DMU services run on
Saturdays in the Summer and on Easter Saturday.
Steam Working: Very little steaming at present –
contact the railway for details.
Prices: Adult £2.40   (unlimited travel
        Child £1.20   on the day of issue
        Family £6.00   with ordinary returns)
Fares and conditions can vary for Special Events.

Detailed Directions by Car:
From All Parts: The railway is situated just off the B4248 between Blaenavon and Brynmawr and is well signposted
as you approach Blaenavon. Use Junction 25A if using the M4 from the East, or Junction 26 from the West. Head
for Pontypool. From the Midlands use the M50, A40 then A465 to Brynmawr. From North & West Wales consider
using the 'Heads of the Valleys' A465 to Brynmawr. As you approach the Railway, look out for the Colliery water
tower – you can't miss it!

RAILWAY PRESERVATION SOCIETY OF IRELAND

Address: Castleview, Whitehead,
Co. Antrim, Northern Ireland BT38 9NA
Telephone Nº: (028) 2826-0803
Year Formed: 1964
Location of Line: Whitehead, Co. Antrim
Length of Line: ¼ mile
Gauge: Irish Standard

Nº of Steam Locos: 9
Nº of Other Locos: 2
Nº of Members: 1,000
Annual Membership Fee: Adult £25.00;
Senior £20.00; Junior £15.00; Family £60.00
Approx Nº of Visitors P.A.: 10,000
Web Site: www.rpsi-online.org
E-mail: rpsitrains@hotmail.com

GENERAL INFORMATION

Nearest NIR Station: Whitehead (½ mile)
Nearest Bus Station: Whitehead (½ mile)
Car Parking: Free parking at site
Coach Parking: Free parking at site
Souvenir Shop(s): Yes
Food & Drinks: Yes

SPECIAL INFORMATION

The Society is the only Main Line Steam Operator in
Ireland.

OPERATING INFORMATION

Opening Times: Sundays in the Summer and also
during Easter and Christmas. There is also a regular
timetable of main line excursions. Phone for further
details.
Steam Working: 2.00pm to 5.00pm at Whitehead
Prices: Depends on the event or the destination of
main line excursions

Detailed Directions by Car:
Whitehead is situated about 15 miles to the North of Belfast just off the A2 between Larne and Carrickfergus. The
location is clearly signposted in Whitehead.

RAVENGLASS & ESKDALE RAILWAY

Address: Ravenglass, Cumbria CA18 1SW **Telephone Nº**: (01229) 717171 **Year Formed**: 1875 **Location**: The Lake District National Park **Length of Line**: 7 miles	**Gauge**: 15 inches **Nº of Steam Locos**: 6 **Nº of Other Locos**: 8 **Nº of Members**: 2,100 **Approx Nº of Visitors P.A.**: 120,000 **Web site**: www.ravenglass-railway.co.uk

GENERAL INFORMATION

Nearest Mainline Station: Ravenglass (adjacent)
Nearest Bus Stop: Ravenglass
Car Parking: Available at both terminals
Coach Parking: At Ravenglass
Souvenir Shop(s): Yes
Food & Drinks: Yes

SPECIAL INFORMATION

From Ravenglass, the Lake District's only coastal village, the line runs through two lovely valleys to the foot of England's highest mountain.

OPERATING INFORMATION

Opening Times: The service runs daily from the end of March until the beginning of November. Also runs during selected weekends in the Winter, Christmas and February half-term. Open from 9.00am to 5.00pm (sometimes later during high season).
Steam Working: Most services are steam hauled.
Prices: Adult £8.20
    Child £4.00
    Family £20.50
    (2 adults + 2 children)

Detailed Directions by Car:
The railway is situated just off the main A595 Western Lake District road.

RHYL MINIATURE RAILWAY

Address: Marine Lake, Wellington Road, Rhyl	**N° of Steam Locos:** 2
	N° of Other Locos: 2
Telephone N°: (01352) 759109	**N° of Members:** Approximately 40
Year Formed: 1911	**Annual Membership Fee:** £7.50
Location of Line: Rhyl	**Approx N° of Visitors P.A.:** 5,000
Length of Line: 1 mile	**Gauge:** 15 inches
	Web site: www.rhylminiaturerailway.co.uk

GENERAL INFORMATION

Nearest Mainline Station: Rhyl (1 mile)
Nearest Bus Station: Rhyl (1 mile)
Car Parking: Car Park opposite the Railway
Coach Parking: Available nearby
Souvenir Shop(s): No
Food & Drinks: Available nearby

SPECIAL INFORMATION

The trust runs the oldest Miniature Railway in the UK. The principal locomotive and train have been operating there since the 1920's.

OPERATING INFORMATION

Opening Times: Bank holiday Sundays and Mondays; every Sunday from 13th June to 12th September; every Thursday from 2nd July to 26th August; every Saturday from 31st July to 26th August. Trains run from 1.00pm to 5.00pm.
Steam Working: All above dates, weather permitting.
Prices: Adult £1.00
         Child £1.00

Detailed Directions by Car:
From All Parts: The Railway is located behind the Ocean Beach Funfair at the west end of Rhyl Promenade.

ROMNEY, HYTHE & DYMCHURCH RAILWAY

Address: New Romney Station, New Romney, Kent TN28 8PL	**N° of Steam Locos**: 11
Telephone N°: (01797) 362353	**N° of Other Locos**: 5
Year Formed: 1927	**N° of Members**: 2,500
Location of Line: Approximately 4 miles south of Folkestone	**Annual Membership Fee**: Supporters association – Adult £14.00; Junior £7.50
Length of Line: 13½ miles	**Approx N° of Visitors P.A.**: 160,000
	Gauge: 15 inches

GENERAL INFORMATION

Nearest Mainline Station: Folkestone Central (4 miles)
Nearest Bus Station: Folkestone (then take bus to Hythe)
Car Parking: Available at all major stations
Coach Parking: At New Romney & Dungeness
Souvenir Shop(s): Yes – 4 at various stations
Food & Drinks: 2 Cafes serving food and drinks

SPECIAL INFORMATION

Opened in 1927 as 'The World's Smallest Public Railway'. Now the only 15" gauge tourist main line railway in the world. Double track, 6 stations.

OPERATING INFORMATION

Opening Times: A daily service runs from 1st April to 30th September. Open at weekends in March and October and for Santa Specials in December.
Steam Working: All operational days.
Prices: Depend on length of journey. Maximums:
   Adult £9.80
   Child £4.90
   Family £29.90 (2 adult + 3 children)

Web Site: www.rhdr.org.uk

Detailed Directions by Car:
Exit the M20 at Junction 11 then follow signs to Hythe and the brown tourist signs for the railway. Alternatively, Take the A259 to New Romney and follow the brown tourist signs for the railway.

RUDYARD LAKE STEAM RAILWAY

Address: Rudyard Station, Rudyard, Near Leek, Staffordshire ST13 8PF
Telephone Nº: (01995) 672280
Year Formed: 1985
Location: Rudyard to Hunthouse Wood
Length of Line: 1½ miles

Nº of Steam Locos: 3
Nº of Other Locos: 2
Nº of Members: –
Approx Nº of Visitors P.A.: 25,000
Gauge: 10¼ inches
Web site: www.rudyardlakerailway.co.uk

GENERAL INFORMATION

Nearest Mainline Station: Stoke-on-Trent (10 miles)
Nearest Bus Station: Leek
Car Parking: Free parking at Rudyard Station
Coach Parking: Free parking at Rudyard Station
Souvenir Shop(s): Yes
Food & Drinks: Yes – Cafe at Dam Station

SPECIAL INFORMATION

The Railway runs along the side of the historic Rudyard Lake that gave author Rudyard Kipling his name. A Steamboat also plies the lake at times.

OPERATING INFORMATION

Opening Times: Every Sunday and Bank Holiday from mid-March to the end of October. Also open on every Saturday from 1st May to 30th September.
Steam Working: All trains are normally steam hauled. Trains run from 11.00am on Sundays and Bank Holidays and from 1.00pm on Saturdays. The last train runs at 4.20pm.
Prices: Adult Return £3.00
        Child Return £1.50
A variety of other fares are also available.

Detailed Directions by Car:
From All Parts: Head for Leek then follow the A523 North towards Macclesfield for 1 mile. Follow the brown tourist signs to the B5331 signposted for Rudyard for ½ mile. Pass under the Railway bridge and turn immediately left and go up the ramp to the Station car park.

RUISLIP LIDO RAILWAY

Address: Reservoir Road, Ruislip, Middlesex HA4 7TY	**Nº of Steam Locos:** 1
Telephone Nº: (01895) 622595	**Nº of Other Locos:** 4
Year Formed: 1979	**Nº of Members:** 155
Location of Line: Ruislip Lido to Woody Bay	**Annual Membership Fee:** £15.00
	Approx Nº of Visitors P.A.: 60,000
Length of Line: 1¼ miles	**Gauge:** 12 inches
	Web site: http://rlr.digiserv.net/

GENERAL INFORMATION

Nearest Mainline Station: West Ruislip (2 miles)
Nearest Bus Station: Ruislip
Car Parking: Available at the Lido
Coach Parking: Available at the Lido
Souvenir Shop(s): Yes
Food & Drinks: A Cafe is open on Sundays and Bank Holidays only.

SPECIAL INFORMATION

The steam locomotive, 'Mad Bess' used by Ruislip Lido Railway was actually built by the members over a 12 year period!

OPERATING INFORMATION

Opening Times: Weekends from mid-February to the end of May and also daily during school holidays. Also open on weekends from September to November and on Sundays in December.
Steam Working: Sundays and Bank Holidays from July to the end of September and also Santa Specials.
Prices: Adult £3.00
Child £3.00

Detailed Directions by Car:
From All Parts: Follow the signs from the A40 and take the A4180 through Ruislip before turning left onto the B469.

RUTLAND RAILWAY MUSEUM

Address: Cottesmore Iron Ore Mines Siding, Ashwell Road, Cottesmore, Oakham, Rutland LE15 7BX	**Length of Line**: ½ mile
	Nº of Steam Locos: 13
	Nº of Other Locos: 26
Telephone Nº: (01572) 813203	**Nº of Members**: 150
Year Formed: 1979	**Annual Membership Fee**: £8.00
Location of Line: Between the villages of Cottesmore and Ashwell	**Approx Nº of Visitors P.A.**: 8,000
	Gauge: Standard

GENERAL INFORMATION

Nearest Mainline Station: Oakham (4 miles)
Nearest Bus Station: Cottesmore or Ashwell (both 1½ miles)
Car Parking: Available at the site
Coach Parking: Limited space available
Souvenir Shop(s): On operating days
Food & Drinks: On operating days only

SPECIAL INFORMATION

The Museum is located at the end of the former Ashwell-Cottesmore mineral branch and is based at the former exchange sidings.

OPERATING INFO

Opening Times: Most weekends throughout the year for static viewing. 11.00am to 5.00pm
Steam Working: 11th/12th April; 2nd/3rd/30th/31st May; 13th June; 29th/30th August; 26th September; 5th/12th/19th December.
Prices: Adult £3.00
Child £2.00 (no charge for under 5's)
Family £8.00
Prices are for admission to the site on steam operating days only. Admission is free at other times. Special prices apply to Santa Specials in December.

Detailed Directions by Car:
From All Parts: The Museum is situated 4 miles north of Oakham between Ashwell and Cottesmore. Follow the brown tourist signs from the B668 Oakham to A1 road or the signs from the A606 Stamford to Oakham Road.

SCOTTISH INDUSTRIAL RAILWAY CENTRE

Address: Dunaskin Open Air Museum, Waterside, Patna, Ayrshire   KA6 7JF
Telephone Nº: (01292) 531144 (Weekdays) (01292) 313579 (Evenings & Weekends)
Year Formed: 1974
Location of Line: Dunaskin Ironworks
Length of Line: A third of a mile

Nº of Steam Locos: 9
Nº of Other Locos: 26
Nº of Members: 180
Annual Membership Fee: £10.00
Approx Nº of Visitors P.A.: 3,500
Gauge: Standard
Web site: www.arpg.org.uk

GENERAL INFORMATION

Nearest Mainline Station: Ayr (10 miles)
Nearest Bus Station: ½ hourly bus service from Ayr – phone (01292) 613500 for more information
Car Parking: Free parking available at the site
Coach Parking: Free parking available at the site
Souvenir Shop(s): Yes
Food & Drinks: Cafe on site

SPECIAL INFORMATION

The Railway is now located at the Dunaskin Open Air Museum based on the preserved site of Europe's best remaining example of a Victorian Ironworks. In addition to the Railway, there are a number of other attractions on the site.

OPERATING INFORMATION

Opening Times: April to October 10.00am to 5.00pm and by request during the winter. Special events take place throughout the year.
Steam Working: Sundays in July and August plus the first Sunday in September. 11.00am to 4.30pm.
Prices: Adult £2.50
          Child £1.50
          Family Tickets £6.00

Detailed Directions by Car:
From All Parts: Dunaskin Open Air Museum is located adjacent to the A713 Ayr to Castle Douglas road.

SEVERN VALLEY RAILWAY

Address: Railway Station, Bewdley, Worcestershire DY12 1BG	**N° of Steam Locos**: 27
Telephone N°: (01299) 403816	**N° of Other Locos**: 12
Year Formed: 1965	**N° of Members**: 13,000
Location of Line: Kidderminster (Worcs.) to Bridgnorth (Shropshire)	**Annual Membership Fee**: Adult £13.00
	Approx N° of Passengers P.A.: 248,000
	Gauge: Standard
Length of Line: 16 miles	**Web site**: www.svr.co.uk

GENERAL INFORMATION

Nearest Mainline Station: Kidderminster (adjacent)
Nearest Bus Station: Kidderminster (500 yards)
Car Parking: Large car park at Kidderminster.
Spaces also available at other stations.
Coach Parking: At Kidderminster
Souvenir Shop(s): At Kidderminster & Bridgnorth
Food & Drinks: Yes – on most trains. Also at
Kidderminster, Bewdley and Bridgnorth

SPECIAL INFORMATION

The SVR has numerous special events including an
Autumn Steam Gala, 1940's weekend, Classic Car &
Bike Day and visits by Thomas the Tank Engine and
Santa!

OPERATING INFORMATION

Opening Times: Weekends throughout the year.
Also daily from 8th May to 26th September and
during local School Holidays.
Steam Working: Train times vary depending on
timetable information. Phone for details.
Prices: Vary depending on the journey taken:
Family Day Rover £29.00
(2 adults + 4 children)

Detailed Directions by Car:
For Kidderminster take M5 and exit Junction 3 or Junction 6. Follow the brown tourist signs for the railway;
From the South: Take the M40 then M42 to Junction 1 for the A448 from Bromsgrove to Kidderminster.

SITTINGBOURNE & KEMSLEY LIGHT RAILWAY

Address: P.O. Box 300, Sittingbourne,
Kent ME10 2DZ
Telephone Nº: (07944) 135033
Talking Timetable: (0871) 222-1568
Year Formed: 1969
Location of Line: North of Sittingbourne
Length of Line: 2 miles

Nº of Steam Locos: 8
Nº of Other Locos: 3
Nº of Members: 250
Annual Membership Fee: £13.00
Approx Nº of Visitors P.A.: 10,000
Gauge: 2 feet 6 inches
Web site: www.sklr.net

GENERAL INFORMATION

Nearest Mainline Station: Sittingbourne (¼ mile)
Nearest Bus Station: Sittingbourne Mainline station
Car Parking: Available at Sittingbourne Station
Coach Parking: Available at Sittingbourne Station
Souvenir Shop(s): Yes
Food & Drinks: Yes

SPECIAL INFORMATION

The railway is the only preserved narrow gauge
steam railway in S.E. England (formerly the
Bowaters Paper Company Railway).

OPERATING INFORMATION

Opening Times: 28th March to 26th September,
Sundays and Bank Holiday weekends. Also open on
Wednesdays in the School holidays.
Steam Working: Trains run from 1.00pm normally,
but from 11.00am on Bank Holidays weekends and
Sundays in August. Last train runs at 4.00pm.
Prices: Adult Return £4.00
         Child Return £2.00
         Senior Citizen Return £3.00
         Family Return £11.00

Detailed Directions by Car:
From East or West: Take the M2 (or M20) to A249 and travel towards Sittingbourne. Take the A2 to Sittingbourne
town and continue to the roundabout outside the Mainline station. Take the turning onto the B2006 (Milton
Regis) and the car park entrance for the Railway is by the next roundabout, behind McDonalds.

SNOWDON MOUNTAIN RAILWAY

Address: Llanberis, Caernarfon, Gwynedd, Wales LL55 4TY	**Length of Line**: 4¾ miles
Telephone Nº: (0870) 458-0033	**Nº of Steam Locos**: 5
Fax Nº: (01286) 872518	**Nº of Other Locos**: 4 + 3 Railcars
Year Formed: 1894	**Nº of Members**: –
Location of Line: Llanberis to Snowdon summit	**Approx Nº of Visitors P.A.**: 130,000
	Gauge: 2 feet 7½ inches
	Web site: www.snowdonrailway.co.uk

GENERAL INFORMATION

Nearest Mainline Station: Bangor (9 miles)
Nearest Bus Station: Caernarfon (7½ miles)
Car Parking: Llanberis Station car park – pay and display. Also other car parks nearby
Coach Parking: As above but space is very limited at busy times.
Souvenir Shop(s): Yes
Food & Drinks: Yes

SPECIAL INFORMATION

Britain's only public rack and pinion mountain railway. Climbs over 3,000 feet to Snowdon summit. Round trip approximately 2½ hours. From mid-March to mid-May, the final section to the summit is closed and trains terminate lower down the mountain. Reduced fares then apply. Take a coat!

OPERATING INFORMATION

Opening Times: Open daily (weather permitting) from 15th March to 1st November. Trains run from 9.00am until mid/late afternoon. Subject to passenger demand.
Steam Working: Normally at least one steam loco on passenger service, but not guaranteed early or late in the season.
Prices: Adult £20.00   Child £15.00
Special rates are available for groups of 15 or more people.

Detailed Directions by Car:
Llanberis Station is situated on the A4086 Caernarfon to Capel Curig road, 7½ miles from Caernarfon. Convenient access via the main North Wales coast road (A55). Exit at the A55/A5 junction and follow signs to Llanberis via B4366, B4547 and A4086.

SOUTH DEVON RAILWAY

Address: Buckfastleigh Station, Buckfastleigh, Devon   TQ11 0DZ
Telephone Nº: (0845) 345-1427
Year Formed: 1969
Location of Line: Totnes to Buckfastleigh via Staverton
Length of Line: 7 miles

Nº of Steam Locos: 16
Nº of Other Locos: 7
Nº of Members: 1,300
Annual Membership Fee: £14.00
Approx Nº of Visitors P.A.: 80,000
Gauge: Standard
Web Site: www.southdevonrailway.org

GENERAL INFORMATION

Nearest Mainline Station: Totnes (¼ mile)
Nearest Bus Station: Totnes (½ mile), Buckfastleigh (Station Road)
Car Parking: Free parking at Buckfastleigh, Council/BR parking at Totnes
Coach Parking: As above
Souvenir Shop(s): Yes – Buckfastleigh & on train
Food & Drinks: Yes – at Buckfastleigh & on train

SPECIAL INFORMATION

The railway was opened in 1872 as the Totnes, Buckfastleigh & Ashburton Railway.

OPERATING INFORMATION

Opening Times: Daily from 3rd April to 31st October.
Steam Working: Almost all trains are steam hauled
Prices: Adult £8.00
  Child £4.80
  Family £23.00 (2 adults + 2 children)
N.B. Extra discounts are available for large groups

Detailed Directions by Car:
Buckfastleigh is half way between Exeter and Plymouth on the A38 Devon Expressway. Totnes can be reached by taking the A385 from Paignton and Torquay. Brown tourist signs give directions for the railway.

SOUTH DOWNS LIGHT RAILWAY

Address: South Downs Light Railway, Stopham Road, Pulborough RH20 1DS	**Nº of Steam Locos**: 10
Telephone Nº: (07711) 717470	**Nº of Other Locos**: 3
Year Formed: 1999	**Nº of Members**: 50
Location: Pulborough Garden Centre	**Annual Membership Fee**: Adult £20.00
Length of Line: ½ mile	**Approx Nº of Visitors P.A.**: 14,000
	Gauge: 10¼ inches

GENERAL INFORMATION

Nearest Mainline Station: Pulborough (½ mile)
Nearest Bus Station: Bus stop just outside Centre
Car Parking: Free parking on site
Coach Parking: Free parking on site
Souvenir Shop(s): Yes
Food & Drinks: Yes – in the Garden Restaurant

SPECIAL INFORMATION

The members of the Society own and operate the largest collection of 10¼ inch gauge scale locomotives in the UK. The Railway is sited/run in conjunction with the Pulborough Garden Centre.

OPERATING INFORMATION

Opening Times: Weekends and Bank Holidays from Easter until mid-September.
Steam Working: Most services are steam hauled except on alternating Saturdays. Phone for details.
Prices: Adult £1.00
           Child £0.70
Under 3's travel free of charge.
Supersaver ticket provides 12 rides for the price of 10.

Web site: www.sdlrs.com

Detailed Directions by Car:
From All Parts: The Centre is situated on the A283, ½ mile west of Pulborough. Pulborough itself is on the A29 London to Bognor Regis Road.

SOUTH TYNEDALE RAILWAY

Address: The Railway Station, Alston, Cumbria CA9 3JB **Telephone Nº:** (01434) 381696 (Enquiries) (01434) 382828 (Talking timetable) **Year Formed:** 1973 **Location of Line:** From Alston, northwards along South Tyne Valley to Kirkhaugh	**Length of Line:** 2¼ miles **Nº of Steam Locos:** 4 **Nº of Other Locos:** 5 **Nº of Members:** 290 **Annual Membership Fee:** £12.00 **Approx Nº of Visitors P.A.:** 22,000 **Gauge:** 2 feet

GENERAL INFORMATION

Nearest Mainline Station: Haltwhistle
(15 miles)
Nearest Bus Station: Alston Townfoot
(¼ mile)
Car Parking: Free parking at Alston Station
Coach Parking: Free parking at Alston Station
Souvenir Shop(s): Yes
Food & Drinks: Yes

Web site: www.strps.org.uk

OPERATING INFORMATION

Opening Times: Bank Holidays and Weekends from Easter until the end of October. Open daily from 19th July to 31st August. Also open Tuesday to Thursday in July and some days in October – contact the Railway for further details.
Steam Working: Varies, but generally Sundays and Bank Holidays throughout the Summer & December weekends. Also daily from 19th July to 31st August.
Prices: Adult Return £5.00; Single £3.00
              Child Return £2.00; Single £1.50
              Children under 3 travel free
              Adult All Day Ticket £12.50
              Child All Day Ticket £5.00

Detailed Directions by Car:
Alston can be reached by a number of roads from various directions including A689, A686 and the B6277. Alston Station is situated just off the A686 Hexham road, north of Alston Town Centre. Look for the brown tourist signs on roads into Alston.

SPA VALLEY RAILWAY

Address: West Station, Tunbridge Wells, Kent TN2 5QY	**Nº of Steam Locos**: 6
Telephone Nº: (01892) 537715	**Nº of Other Locos**: 8
Year Formed: 1985	**Nº of Members**: Approximately 660
Location of Line: Tunbridge Wells West to Eridge (currently to Groombridge)	**Annual Membership Fee**: £15.00
	Approx Nº of Visitors P.A.: 20,000
	Gauge: Standard
Length of Line: 3½ miles operational	**Web Site**: www.spavalleyrailway.co.uk

GENERAL INFORMATION

Nearest Mainline Station: Tunbridge Wells Central (½ mile)
Nearest Bus Stop: Outside Sainsbury's (100yds)
Car Parking: Available nearby
Coach Parking: Coach station in Montacute Road (150 yards)
Souvenir Shop(s): Yes
Food & Drinks: Yes

SPECIAL INFORMATION

The Railway's Tunbridge Wells Terminus is in a historic and unique L.B. & S.C.R. engine shed. The Railway's aims are to extend to Eridge to connect with the Main Line.

OPERATING INFORMATION

Opening Times: Weekends from 27th March to 31st October. Some weekdays during School Holidays and also Santa Specials in December.
Steam Working: Most services are steam-hauled. Trains run from 10.30am to 4.15pm.
Prices: Adult Return £4.00
Child/Senior Citizen Return £3.00
Unlimited Day Travel £6.00
Family Return £12.00 (2 adult + 2 child)
Parties of 20 or more are charged at £3.50 per head.

Detailed Directions by Car:
The Spa Valley Railway is in the southern part of Tunbridge Wells, 100 yards off the A26. Station is adjacent to Sainsbury's and Homebase. Car Parks are nearby in Major Yorks Road, Union House & Linden Close.

STEAM – MUSEUM OF THE GREAT WESTERN RAILWAY

Address: Steam – Museum of the Great Western Railway, Kemble Drive, Swindon   SN2 2TA
Telephone Nº: (01793) 466646
Year Formed: 2000

Nº of Steam Locos: 6
Nº of Other Locos: 1
Approx Nº of Visitors P.A.: 100,000
Web site: www.steam-museum.org.uk

GENERAL INFORMATION

Nearest Mainline Station: Swindon (10 min. walk)
Nearest Bus Station: Swindon (10 minute walk)
Car Parking: Ample parking space available in the Outlet Centre (charges apply)
Coach Parking: Free parking on site
Souvenir Shop(s): Yes
Food & Drinks: Yes

SPECIAL INFORMATION

Voted Wiltshire's Family Attraction of the Year, STEAM tells the story of the men and women who built the Great Western Railway.

OPERATING INFORMATION

Opening Times: Open all year round from 10.00am to 5.00pm Monday to Saturday, 11.00am to 5.00pm on Sundays. Special Events: 18th & 19th September – Great Western Steam Convention.
Steam Working: –
Prices: Adult Tickets £5.95
    Child Tickets £3.80
    Family Tickets £14.70
    Senior Citizen Tickets £3.90
    Children under 5 are admitted free

Detailed Directions by Car:
Exit the M4 at Junction 16 and follow the brown tourist signs to 'Outlet Centre'. Similarly follow the brown signs from all other major routes.   From the Railway Station: STEAM is a short walk and is accessible through the pedestrian tunnel – entrance by Emlyn Square.

STRATHSPEY STEAM RAILWAY

Address: Aviemore Station, Dalfaber Road, Aviemore, Inverness-shire, PH22 1PY **Telephone Nº**: (01479) 810725 **Year Formed**: 1971 **Location of Line**: Aviemore to Boat of Garten and Broomhill, Inverness-shire	**Length of Line**: 9½ miles at present **Gauge**: Standard **Nº of Steam Locos**: 7 **Nº of Other Locos**: 10 **Nº of Members**: 800 **Annual Membership Fee**: £16.00 **Approx Nº of Visitors P.A.**: 45,000

GENERAL INFO

Nearest Mainline Station: Aviemore – Strathspey trains depart from Platform 3
Nearest Bus Station: Aviemore (600 yds)
Car Parking: Available at all stations
Coach Parking: Available at Aviemore and Boat of Garten Stations
Souvenir Shop(s): Yes – at Aviemore and Boat of Garten Stations
Food & Drinks: Available on Steam trains only (except on Saturdays)

SPECIAL INFO

The railway now operates from Aviemore Station. In the waiting room, there is a small exhibition about the history of the line between Aviemore & Inverness and about the renovation of the station. The Railway was extended to Broomhill Station in 2002 and features in the BBC series 'Monarch of the Glen'.

OPERATING INFO

Opening Times: Daily from 24th May to 30th September. Restricted days in October and other dates in December. Phone for details. Generally open from 9.30am to 4.30pm.
Steam Working: Most trains are steam-hauled but diesel power is used whenever necessary. Phone the Railway for details.
Prices: Adult Return £8.40
                 Child Return £4.20
                 Family Return £21.00
                 (2 adults + up to 3 children)
Day Rover tickets are available

Web site: www.strathspeyrailway.co.uk

Detailed Directions by Car:
For Aviemore Station from South: Take the A9 then B970 and turn left between the railway & river bridges. For Boat of Garten from North; Take the A9 then A938 to Carr Bridge, then B9153 and A95 and follow the signs; From North East: Take A95 to Boat of Garten.

SWANAGE RAILWAY

Address: Station House, Railway Station, Swanage, Dorset BH19 1HB
Telephone Nº: (01929) 425800
Year Formed: 1976
Location of Line: Swanage to Norden
Length of Line: 6 miles
Gauge: Standard

Nº of Steam Locos: 5
Nº of Other Locos: 5
Nº of Members: 4,200
Annual Membership Fee: Adult £15.00; Junior/Senior Citizens £9.00; Family 30.00
Approx Nº of Visitors P.A.: 191,397 (exact figures for 2002)
Web site: www.swanagerailway.co.uk

GENERAL INFORMATION

Nearest Mainline Station: Wareham (10 miles)
Nearest Bus Station: Swanage Station (adjacent)
Car Parking: Park & Ride at Norden. Public car parks in Swanage (5 minutes walk)
Coach Parking: Available at Norden
Souvenir Shop(s): Yes – at Swanage Station
Food & Drinks: Yes – buffet available on trains and also Swanage Station Buffet and at Norden.

SPECIAL INFORMATION

The railway runs along part of the route of the old Swanage to Wareham railway, opened in 1885.

OPERATING INFORMATION

Opening Times: Weekends throughout the year and daily from April to October. Opens from 9.30am to 5.00pm.
Steam Working: All services are steam-hauled
Prices: Adult £7.00
Child £5.00
Family £20.00

Detailed Directions by Car:
Norden Park & Ride Station is situated off the A351 on the approach to Corfe Castle. Swanage Station is situated in the centre of the town, just a few minutes walk from the beach. Take the A351 to reach Swanage.

SWANSEA VALE RAILWAY

Address: Upper Bank Works, Pentrechwyth, Swansea SA1 7DB	**Nº of Steam Locos**: 5
Telephone Nº: (01792) 461000	**Nº of Other Locos**: 5
Year Formed: 1980	**Nº of Members**: 150
Location of Line: Six Pit Junction, Llansamlet, Swansea	**Annual Membership Fee**: £10.00
	Approx Nº of Visitors P.A.: 5,000
Length of Line: ¾ mile	**Gauge**: Standard
	Web: homepage.ntlworld.com/michael.meyrick

GENERAL INFORMATION

Nearest Mainline Station: Llansamlet (¾ mile)
Nearest Bus Station: Swansea Quadrant (3 miles)
Car Parking: 150 spaces available at the site
Coach Parking: 3 spaces available at the site
Souvenir Shop(s): Yes – on the trains
Food & Drinks: Light snacks are available on trains

SPECIAL INFORMATION

The line is due to be extended to 1¼ miles in the Autumn of 1999. Also, guided tours can be arranged at £1.00 per head to view the shed, old turntable base and ash pit.

OPERATING INFORMATION

Opening Times: Saturdays between April and September. Also Bank Holidays and a number of other dates. Not always a steam service. Contact the railway for more complete information. Services run from 12.00pm to 4.00pm.
Steam Working: Certain dates only, although most running days in the Summer are Steam days. Contact the railway for more information.
Prices: Adult £3.00
     Child £2.00
     Family £10.00
Pay once – ride all day.
Prices may change for special events.

Detailed Directions by Car:
From the East: Exit the M4 at Junction 44 (Swansea East), follow signs for Llansamlet and Morriston. At the third set of traffic lights turn left and look for the steam loco signs; From the West: Exit the M4 at Junction 45 (Morriston) then follow signs for Llansamlet; From City Centre: Cross the river near Parc Tawe Shopping Centre, follow signs to Llansamlet on A4217 for 3 miles. Pass the Colliers Arms on the left, pass under the main line railway bridge and turn next left.

SWINDON & CRICKLADE RAILWAY

Address: Blunsdon Station, Tadpole Lane, Blunsdon, Swindon, Wilts   SN25 2DA
Phone Nº: (01793) 771615
Year Formed: 1978
Location of Line: Blunsdon to Hayes Knoll
Length of Line: ¾ mile

Nº of Steam Locos: 8
Nº of Other Locos: 7
Nº of Members: 500
Annual Membership Fee: £10.00
Approx Nº of Visitors P.A.: 8,500
Gauge: Standard

GENERAL INFORMATION

Nearest Mainline Station: Swindon (5 miles)
Nearest Bus Station: Bus stop at Oakhurst (¾ mile)
Car Parking: Free parking at Blunsdon Station
Coach Parking: Free parking at Blunsdon Station
Souvenir Shop(s): Yes
Food & Drinks: Yes

SPECIAL INFORMATION

The Engine Shed at Hayes Knoll Station is now open to the public.

Web site: www.swindon-cricklade-railway.org

OPERATING INFORMATION

Opening Times: The Railway is open every weekend and Bank Holidays for viewing only. Santa Specials in December and other various special events throughout the year have Steam train rides. Open 11.00am to 4.00pm. Diesel trains run every Sunday.
Steam Working: Certain dates only – contact the railway for further details.
Prices: Adult £3.50
           Child £2.50
           Family £10.00
Prices are different for special events.

Detailed Directions by Car:
From the M4: Exit the M4 at Junction 15 and follow the A419. After the roundabout by the Little Chef, turn left at the next set of traffic lights towards Blunsdon Stadium and follow the signs: From Cirencester: Follow the A419 to the traffic lights at the top of Blunsdon Hill, then turn right and follow signs for the railway.

TALYLLYN RAILWAY

Address: Wharf Station, Tywyn, Gwynedd, LL36 9EY	**Nº of Steam Locos**: 6
Telephone Nº: (01654) 710472	**Nº of Other Locos**: 4
Year Formed: 1865	**Nº of Members**: 3,500
Location of Line: Tywyn to Nant Gwernol Station	**Annual Membership Fee**: Adult £20.00
	Approx Nº of Visitors P.A.: 50,000
Length of Line: 7¼ miles	**Gauge**: 2 feet 3 inches
	Web site: www.talyllyn.co.uk

GENERAL INFORMATION

Nearest Mainline Station: Tywyn (300 yards)
Nearest Bus Station: Tywyn (300 yards)
Car Parking: 100 yards away
Coach Parking: Free parking (100 yards)
Souvenir Shop(s): Yes
Food & Drinks: Yes

SPECIAL INFORMATION

Talyllyn Railway was the first preserved railway in the world – saved from closure in 1951. The railway was opened in 1866 to carry slate from Bryn Eglwys Quarry to Tywyn.

OPERATING INFORMATION

Opening Times: Daily from 28th March to 6th November. Generally open from 10.00am to 5.00pm (later during the summer).
Steam Working: All passenger trains are steam-hauled.
Prices: Adult Return £10.00 (Day Rover ticket) Children (ages 5-15) pay £2.00 if travelling with an adult. Otherwise, they pay half adult fare. Children under the age of 5 travel free of charge.
The fares shown above are for a full round trip. Tickets to intermediate stations are cheaper.

Detailed Directions by Car:
From the North: Take the A493 from Dolgellau into Tywyn; From the South: Take the A493 from Machynlleth to Tywyn.

TANFIELD RAILWAY

Address: Marley Hill Engine Shed, Old Marley Hill, Gateshead, Tyne & Wear NE16 5ET	**Length of Line**: 3 miles
	Nº of Steam Locos: 25
	Nº of Other Locos: 9
Telephone Nº: (0191) 388-7545	**Nº of Members**: 150
Fax Nº: (0191) 387-4784	**Annual Membership Fee**: £8.00
Year Formed: 1976	**Approx Nº of Visitors P.A.**: 40,000
Location of Line: Between Sunniside & East Tanfield, Co. Durham	**Gauge**: Standard
	Web site: www.tanfield-railway.co.uk

GENERAL INFORMATION

Nearest Mainline Station: Newcastle-upon-Tyne (8 miles)
Nearest Bus St'n: Gateshead Interchange (6 miles)
Car Parking: Spaces for 150 cars at Andrews House and 100 spaces at East Tanfield
Coach Parking: Spaces for 6 or 7 coaches only
Souvenir Shop(s): Yes
Food & Drinks: Yes – light snacks only

SPECIAL INFORMATION

Tanfield Railway is the oldest existing railway in use – it was originally opened in 1725. It also runs beside The Causey Arch, the oldest railway bridge in the world.

OPERATING INFORMATION

Opening Times: Every Sunday & Bank Holiday Monday throughout the year. Also opens on Wednesdays & Thursdays in Summer school holidays.
Steam Working: Trains run 11.00am to 4.00pm (11.30am to 3.15pm in the Winter).
Prices: Adult £5.00
Child £2.50 (Under 5's travel free)
Senior Citizen £3.50
Family £12.50 (2 adults + 2 children)

Detailed Directions by Car:
Sunniside Station is off the A6076 Sunniside to Stanley road in Co. Durham. To reach the Railway, leave A1(M), follow signs for Beamish museum at Chester-le-Street then continue to Stanley and follow Tanfield Railway signs.

TEIFI VALLEY RAILWAY

Address: Henllan Station, Henllan, near Newcastle Emlyn, Carmarthenshire **Telephone Nº**: (01559) 371077 **Year Formed**: 1972 **Location of Line**: Between Cardigan and Carmarthen off the A484 **Length of Line**: 2 miles	**Nº of Steam Locos**: 2 **Nº of Other Locos**: 3 **Nº of Members**: Approximately 150 **Annual Membership Fee**: £12.00 **Approx Nº of Visitors P.A.**: 15,000 **Gauge**: 2 feet **Web site**: www.teifivalleyrailway.co.uk

GENERAL INFORMATION

Nearest Mainline Station: Carmarthen (10 miles)
Nearest Bus Station: Carmarthen (10 miles)
Car Parking: Spaces for 70 cars available.
Coach Parking: Spaces for 4 coaches available.
Souvenir Shop(s): Yes
Food & Drinks: Yes (snacks only)

SPECIAL INFORMATION

The Railway was formerly part of the G.W.R. but now runs on a Narrow Gauge using Quarry Engines.

OPERATING INFORMATION

Opening Times: Open daily from 1st May until the end of October (closed most Fridays and Saturdays). Open every day from 14th July to 5th September. Open on some days in December for 'Santa Specials'. Open 10.00am – 3.30pm when the last train departs.
Steam Working: Occasional steam working – please phone the Railway for details.
Prices: Adult £5.00
          Child £3.00
          Senio Citizens £4.00
A 10% discount is available for parties of 10 or more.

Detailed Directions by Car:
From All Parts: The Railway is situated in the Village of Henllan between the A484 and the A475 (on the B4334) about 4 miles east of Newcastle Emlyn.

TELFORD STEAM RAILWAY

Address: The Old Loco Shed, Bridge Road, Horsehay, Telford, Shropshire
Telephone Nº: (01952) 503880
Enquiries: (07765) 858348
Year Formed: 1976
Location of Line: Based at Horsehay & Dawley Station

Length of Line: ½ mile standard gauge, an eighth of a mile 2 foot narrow gauge
Nº of Steam Locos: 5
Nº of Other Locos: 12
Nº of Members: Approximately 220
Annual Membership Fee: £8.50
Approx Nº of Visitors P.A.: 10,000

GENERAL INFORMATION

Nearest Mainline Station: Wellington or Telford Central
Nearest Bus Station: Dawley (1 mile)
Car Parking: Free parking at the site
Coach Parking: Free parking at the site
Souvenir Shop(s): 'Freight Stop Gift Shop'
Food & Drinks: 'The Furnaces' Tea Room

SPECIAL INFORMATION

Telford Steam Railway has both a Standard Gauge and Narrow Gauge line as well as Miniature and Model Railways.

OPERATING INFORMATION

Opening Times: Every Sunday and Bank Holiday between Easter and the end of September. Santa Specials run in December. Open 11.00am to 4.00pm except Bank Holidays when it is open until 5.00pm
Steam Working: 2 foot gauge on all operating days. Standard gauge on the last Sunday of the month, every Sunday in August and also on Bank Holidays.
Prices: Adult all day tickets £3.50
Child all day tickets £2.50

Web site: www.telfordsteamrailway.co.uk

Detailed Directions by Car:
From All Parts: Exit the M54 at Junction 6 and follow the brown tourist signs for the railway.

VALE OF GLAMORGAN RAILWAY

Address: Barry Island Station, Barry Island, Vale of Glamorgan CF62 5TH
Telephone Nº: (01446) 748816
Year Formed: 1979 (1994 on present site)
Location of Line: Barry Island
Length of Line: 3 miles

Nº of Steam Locos: 5 (10 in storage)
Nº of Other Locos: 3
Nº of Members: 275
Annual Membership Fee: £10.00
Approx Nº of Visitors P.A.: 10,000
Gauge: Standard

GENERAL INFORMATION

Nearest Mainline Station: Barry Island (across the platform)
Nearest Bus Station: Outside station
Car Parking: Large car park (300 yards)
Coach Parking: Car park (300 yards)
Souvenir Shop(s): Yes
Food & Drinks: Yes

SPECIAL INFORMATION

The aim of the company is to portray the rich history of railways in South Wales. A new 1¼ mile extension to the line recently opened.

OPERATING INFORMATION

Opening Times: Weekends from July until early September. Special events will run at Easter and other times throughout the year. Please phone the Railway for further details.
Steam Working: 11.00am to 4.00pm
Prices: Adult £3.00
          Child £2.00
          Family £7.00
          (2 adults + 2 children)

Detailed Directions by Car:
Exit the M4 at Junction 33 and follow the brown tourist signs for the funfair and beach to Barry Island. The station is situated on the left behind the funfair.

VALE OF RHEIDOL RAILWAY

Address: The Locomotive Shed, Park Avenue, Aberystwyth, Dyfed SY23 1PG	**Nº of Steam Locos:** 3
Telephone Nº: (01970) 625819	**Nº of Other Locos:** 1
Year Formed: 1902	**Nº of Members:** None
Location of Line: Aberystwyth to Devil's Bridge	**Annual Membership Fee:** –
	Approx Nº of Visitors P.A.: 37,000
Length of Line: 11¾ miles	**Gauge:** 1 foot 11¾ inches
	Web site: www.rheidolrailway.co.uk

GENERAL INFORMATION

Nearest Mainline Station: Aberystwyth (adjacent)
Nearest Bus Station: Aberystwyth (adjacent)
Car Parking: Available on site
Coach Parking: Parking available 400 yards away
Souvenir Shop(s): Yes
Food & Drinks: Yes

SPECIAL INFORMATION

The journey between the stations take one hour in each direction. At Devil's Bridge there is a cafe, toilets, a picnic area and the famous Mynach Falls. The line climbs over 600 feet in 11¾ miles.

OPERATING INFORMATION

Opening Times: Open almost every day from 3rd April to 30th October with some exceptions. Please phone the railway for further information.
Steam Working: All trains are steam-hauled. Trains run from 10.30am to 4.00pm on most days.
Prices: Adult Return £11.50
Child Return – First 2 children per adult pay £2.50 each. Further children pay £5.75 each

---

Detailed Directions by Car:
From the North take A487 into Aberystwyth. From the East take A470 and A44 to Aberystwyth. From the South take A487 or A485 to Aberystwyth. The Station is joined on to the Mainline Station in Alexandra Road.

WATERWORKS RAILWAY

Address: Kew Bridge Steam Museum, Green Dragon Lane, Brentford, TW8 0EN	**Nº of Steam Locos**: 2
Telephone Nº: (020) 8568-4757	**Nº of Other Locos**: 1
Year Formed: 1986	**Nº of Members**: 650
Location of Line: Greater London	**Annual Membership Fee**: £15.00 Adult
Length of Line: Under 1 mile	**Approx Nº of Visitors P.A.**: 20,000
	Gauge: Narrow

GENERAL INFORMATION

Nearest Mainline Station: Kew Bridge (3 minute walk)
Nearest Bus Station: Bus stop across the road – Services 65, 267 and 237
Car Parking: Spaces for 40 cars available on site
Coach Parking: Available on site – book in advance
Souvenir Shop(s): Yes
Food & Drinks: Yes – at weekends only

SPECIAL INFORMATION

The Museum is a former Victorian Pumping Station with a collection of working Steam Pumping Engines. The Railway demonstrates typical water board use of Railways.

OPERATING INFORMATION

Opening Times: 11.00am to 5.00pm, 7 days a week throughout the year.
Steam Working: Sundays and Bank Holiday Mondays from March to November.
Prices: Adult £5.20
Child £3.00
Senior Citizen £4.20
Family £15.95 (2 adults + 3 children)

Web site: www.kbsm.org

Detailed Directions by Car:
From All Parts: Exit the M4 at Junction 2 and follow the A4 to Chiswick Roundabout. Take the exit signposted for Kew Gardens & Brentford. Go straight on at the next two sets of traffic lights following A315. After 2nd set of lights take the first right for the museum. The museum is next to the tall Victorian tower.

WELLS & WALSINGHAM LIGHT RAILWAY

Address: The Station, Wells-next-the-Sea NR23 1QB
Telephone Nº: (01328) 710631
Year Formed: 1982
Location of Line: Wells-next-the-Sea to Walsingham, Norfolk
Length of Line: 4 miles

Nº of Steam Locos: 1
Nº of Other Locos: 1
Nº of Members: 50
Annual Membership Fee: £11.00
Approx Nº of Visitors P.A.: 20,000
Gauge: 10¼ inches

GENERAL INFORMATION

Nearest Mainline Station: King's Lynn (21 miles)
Nearest Bus Station: Norwich (24 miles)
Car Parking: Free parking at site
Coach Parking: Free parking at site
Souvenir Shop(s): Yes
Food & Drinks: Yes

SPECIAL INFORMATION

The Railway is the longest 10¼ inch narrow-gauge steam railway in the world. The course of the railway is famous for wildlife and butterflies in season.

OPERATING INFORMATION

Opening Times: Daily from Good Friday to the end of October.
Steam Working: Trains run from 10.15am on operating days.
Prices: Adult Return £7.00
Child Return £5.00

Detailed Directions by Car:
Wells-next-the-Sea is situated on the North Norfolk Coast midway between Hunstanton and Cromer. The Main Station is situated on the main A149 Stiffkey Road. Follow the brown tourist signs for the Railway.

WELSH HIGHLAND RAILWAY (CAERNARFON)

Postal Address: Ffestiniog Railway, Harbour Station, Porthmadog LL49 9NF
Telephone Nº: (01766) 516073
Web site: www.festrail.co.uk
Year Formed: 1997
Location: Caernarfon to Rhyd Ddu
Length of Line: 12 miles (in July 2003)

Nº of Steam Locos: 5 (2 working)
Nº of Other Locos: 2
Nº of Members: 1,000
Annual Membership Fee: £20.00
Approx Nº of Visitors P.A.: 70,000
Gauge: 1 foot 11½ inches
Web site: www.festrail.co.uk

GENERAL INFORMATION

Nearest Mainline Station: Bangor (7 miles) (Bus service Nº 5 runs to Caernarfon)
Nearest Bus Station: Caernarfon
Car Parking: Parking available at Caernarfon
Coach Parking: At Victoria Docks (¼ mile)
Souvenir Shop(s): Yes
Food & Drinks: Light refreshments on some trains

SPECIAL INFORMATION

The Railway is being reconstructed between Caernarfon and Porthmadog along the track bed of the original Welsh Highland Railway. A further extension from Waunfawr to Rhyd Ddu is expected to open in July 2003. Please check the Railway web site (shown above) for up to date information.

OPERATING INFORMATION

Opening Times: Daily from 30th March to 31st October + some trains in Winter. Train times vary.
Steam Working: Most trains in the Summer are steam-hauled.
Prices: Adult £14.00 to Rhyd Ddu
　　　　　Child £7.00 to Rhyd Ddu
N.B. One Child is admitted free of charge with every Adult. Also, price reductions are available for Senior Citizens and groups of 20 or more.

Detailed Directions by Car:
Take either the A487(T), the A4085 or the A4086 to Caernarfon then follow the brown tourist signs for the Railway which is situated in St. Helens Road next to the Castle.

WELSH HIGHLAND RAILWAY (PORTHMADOG)

Address: Tremadog Road, Porthmadog, Gwynedd LL49 9DY	**Nº of Steam Locos**: 6
Telephone Nº: (01766) 513402	**Nº of Other Locos**: 20
Year Formed: 1964	**Nº of Members**: 1,000
Location of Line: Porthmadog, Gwynedd LL49 9DY	**Annual Membership Fee**: £15.00 Adult
	Approx Nº of Visitors P.A.: 12,500
Length of Line: ¾ mile	**Gauge**: 1 foot 11½ inches
	Web site: www.whr.co.uk

GENERAL INFORMATION

Nearest Mainline Station: Porthmadog (50 yards)
Nearest Bus Station: Services 1 & 3 stop 200 yards away
Car Parking: Free parking at site, plus a public car park within 100 yards
Coach Parking: Adjacent
Souvenir Shop(s): Yes – large range available.
Food & Drinks: Yes – excellent home cooking!

SPECIAL INFORMATION

The Welsh Highland Railway is a family-orientated attraction based around a Railway Heritage Centre and includes a tour of the sheds. A ½ mile extension to Traeth Mawr is currently being constructed.

OPERATING INFORMATION

Opening Times: 3-18/24/25 April; 1/2/3/8/9/15/16/22/23/29/30/31 May; 1st June to 26th September; 2/3/8/9/10/16/17/23-31 October. Trains run at 10.45am, 11.45am, 1.30pm, 2.30pm, 3.30pm & 4.15pm (last train runs at 3.30 September/October.)
Steam Working: 10-18 April; 1/2/3/29/30/31 May; 1-6/19/20 June; 3/4/10/11/17/18/24-31 July; Daily in August; 4/5/11/12/18/19/25/26 September; 9/10/23-31 October.
Prices: Adult Return £3.75 Child Return £2.50
 Senior Citizen Return £3.00
 Family Return £10.00
 (2 adults + 2 children)
Children under 5 are admitted free of charge

Detailed Directions by Car:
From Bangor/Caernarfon take the A487 to Porthmadog. From Pwllheli take the A497 to Porthmadog then turn left at the roundabout. From the Midlands take A487 to Portmadog. Once in Porthmadog, follow the brown tourist signs. The line is located right next to Porthmadog Mainline Station.

WELSHPOOL & LLANFAIR LIGHT RAILWAY

Address: The Station, Llanfair Caereinion, Powys SY21 0SF	**Nº of Steam Locos:** 8
Telephone Nº: (01938) 810441	**Nº of Other Locos:** 3
Year Formed: 1959	**Nº of Members:** 2,300
Location of Line: Welshpool to Llanfair Caereinion, Mid Wales	**Annual Membership Fee:** £17.50
	Approx Nº of Visitors P.A.: 25,000
	Gauge: 2 feet 6 inches
Length of Line: 8 miles	**Web site:** www.wllr.org.uk

GENERAL INFORMATION

Nearest Mainline Station: Welshpool (1 mile)
Nearest Bus Station: Welshpool (1 mile)
Car Parking: Free parking at Welshpool and Llanfair Caereinion
Coach Parking: As above
Souvenir Shop(s): Yes – at both ends of line
Food & Drinks: Yes – at Llanfair only

SPECIAL INFORMATION

The railway has the steepest gradient of any British railway, reaching a summit of 603 feet.

OPERATING INFORMATION

Opening Times: Easter and Bank Holidays and weekends in April, May and September. Daily from 17th July to 5th September. Most other days in June and July plus dates in September, October and December. Generally open from 9.30am to 6.00pm.
Steam Working: All trains are steam-hauled
Prices: Adult £9.50
      Senior Citizens £8.50
Children under the age of 3 are free of charges. The first child aged 3-15 per adult is charged £1.00. All other children are charged half-price fare of £4.75

Detailed Directions by Car:
Both stations are situated alongside the A458 Shrewsbury to Dolgellau road and are clearly signposted

WEST LANCASHIRE LIGHT RAILWAY

Address: Station Road, Hesketh Bank, Nr. Preston, Lancashire PR4 6SP	**Nº of Steam Locos**: 9
Telephone Nº: (01772) 815881	**Nº of Other Locos**: 24
Year Formed: 1967	**Nº of Members**: Approximately 95
Location of Line: On former site of Alty's Brickworks, Hesketh Bank	**Annual Membership Fee**: £15.00 Adult; £20.00 Family
Length of Line: ¼ mile	**Approx Nº of Visitors P.A.**: 14,000
	Web site: www.westlancs.org

GENERAL INFORMATION

Nearest Mainline Station: Rufford (4 miles)
Nearest Bus Station: Preston (7 miles)
Car Parking: Space for 50 cars at site
Coach Parking: Space for 3 coaches at site
Souvenir Shop(s): Yes
Food & Drinks: Only soft drinks & snacks

SPECIAL INFORMATION

The Railway is run by volunteers and there is a large collection of Industrial Narrow Gauge equipment.

OPERATING INFORMATION

Opening Times: Sundays and Bank Holidays throughout the year. No trains run from November to April (except Santa Specials). Various other Special Events are held during the Summer – phone for details. Trains run from 12.00pm to 5.20pm
Steam Working: Trains operate on Sundays and Bank Holidays from 6th April until the end of October. There are also 'Santa Specials' on the two weekends prior to Christmas.
Prices: Adult £2.00   Child £1.25
Family Tickets £4.50
Senior Citizens £1.50

Detailed Directions by Car:
Travel by the A59 from Liverpool or Preston or by the A565 from Southport to the junction of the two roads at Tarleton. From here follow signs to Hesketh Bank. The Railway is signposted.

WEST SOMERSET RAILWAY

Address: The Railway Station, Minehead, Somerset TA24 5BG	**Nº of Steam Locos:** 9
Telephone Nº: (01643) 704996 (enquiries)	**Nº of Other Locos:** 13
Year Formed: 1976	**Nº of Members:** 4,000
Location of Line: Bishops Lydeard (near Taunton) to Minehead	**Annual Membership Fee:** £15.00
	Approx Nº of Visitors P.A.: 185,000
Length of Line: 19¾ miles	**Gauge:** Standard

GENERAL INFORMATION

Nearest Mainline Station: Taunton (4 miles)
Nearest Bus Station: Taunton (4½ miles) – Services 28, 28A & 928 run to Bishops Lydeard
Car Parking: Free parking at Bishops Lydeard; Council car parking at Minehead
Coach Parking: As above
Souvenir Shop(s): Yes – at Minehead, Bishops Lydeard and Washford
Food & Drinks: Yes – At some stations. Buffet and Dining cars on all trains.

SPECIAL INFORMATION

Britain's longest Heritage railway runs through the Quantock Hills & along Bristol Channel Coast. Ten Stations with museums at Washford & Blue Anchor.

OPERATING INFORMATION

Opening Times: March to December. Daily from May to September. Open 9.30am to 5.30pm
Steam Working: All operatings days except Diesel Galas.
Prices: Adult £10.80
Child £5.50
Family £27.20 (2 adults + 4 children)

Web site: www.west-somerset-railway.co.uk

Detailed Directions by Car:
Exit the M5 at Taunton (Junction 25) and follow signs for A358 to Williton and then the A39 for Minehead. In Minehead, brown tourist signs give directions to the railway.
